'More than half of this hugely power[...] have to have been written, but the f[...] exactly why we should care so much that it had to be. A loving, humorous and clear-eyed portrait of a dude called Laughing Boy, the first half of the book brings vividly to life the reality behind the bland descriptors of "autism" and "learning disability" trotted out by social workers, clinicians and, yes, lawyers. The second half of the book demonstrates just how badly things can go wrong when the system fails to recognise and respond to that individual and their needs, and, harrowingly, how that same system can then conspire to render accountability almost unfeasibly difficult. This is, rightly, a book which makes difficult reading for anyone professionally invested in any part of the system - for exactly the same reasons, it should make compulsory reading.'

– Alex Ruck Keene, barrister,
writer and educator, 39 Essex Chambers

'A truly remarkable book that should never have had to be written, and that should be read by literally anyone who cares about their fellow human being; Sara brings beauty to her narrative, juxtaposed to the brutal ugliness of the subject matter, juxtaposed to the heart wrenching loving memory of a son taken from his family before his time. An emotional roller coaster made even more poignant by reason that the text is so tragically not fictional.'

– Dr Luke Beardon, Senior Lecturer in Autism,
Sheffield Hallam University and author

'This account of a parent's experience brings to light the vital need to really listen, understand and work alongside people with learning disabilities and their families to ensure that care and support is right for them.'

– *Lyn Romeo, Chief Social Worker for Adults*

'Anyone who cares about patient safety and fairness should read this book. It will make you cry, it will make you laugh, it will make you think, and I would be amazed if it did not make you passionate about changing things.'

– *Peter Walsh, Chief Executive,*
Action against Medical Accidents (AvMA)

'The echoes of those who no longer speak…no candy coating, it is what it is; a tragedy born from negligence. To quote: "At the heart of this story is love." Love "mobilised a social movement" and love keeps hope alive. Not a good read, a must read.'

– *Dr Wenn B. Lawson, lecturer and author*

'This is a beautifully written and deeply moving account of a mother's love for her son. It is a book about how a social movement, inspired by the quest for justice, continues to seek accountability and change following Connor Sparrowhawk's needless death. This book deserves to be read widely and for people to take action from it. #JusticeForLB'

– *Rhidian Hughes, Voluntary Organisations Disability Group*

'A searingly powerful book. Dr Ryan fought to discover why her son died. She was determined to hold the individuals and institutions responsible for her son's death to account. Speaking truth to power, challenging and changing cultures. A true champion for weary parents, bringing hope to those who strive for justice.'

– *Sarah Holmes MBE, Patient Advocate*

'I am Gary Bourlet, Co-Founder of the charity Learning Disability England. I have been asked to write something about Sara's book.

When reading the book you will find yourself going through lots of different emotions – you may need to have a hanky ready. You will find yourself laughing at the fun side of Connor, and crying at the tragedy. A child with his life ahead of him, a typical teen who never had the chance to grow into a young man with so much to live for and so much to contribute.

What happened to Connor shows that people with learning disabilities are still not treated as human beings like everyone else. Professionals need to listen to people with learning disabilities and their families and friends about what their care should be. There is a good way to sum this up - "Nothing about us without us".'

– *Gary Bourlet, Founder of Learning Disability England and self-advocate of learning disabled rights*

Justice for Laughing Boy

of related interest

Hidden Cameras
Everything You Need to Know About Covert Recording,
Undercover Recording and Secret Filming
Joe Plomin
ISBN 978 1 84905 643 4
eISBN 978 1 78450 136 5

How We Treat the Sick
Neglect and Abuse in Our Health Services
Michael Mandelstam
ISBN 978 1 84905 160 6
eISBN 978 0 85700 355 3

Betraying the NHS
Health Abandoned
Michael Mandelstam
ISBN 978 1 84310 482 7
eISBN 978 1 84642 569 1

Learning from Baby P
The politics of blame, fear and denial
Sharon Shoesmith
ISBN 978 1 78592 003 5
eISBN 978 1 78450 238 6

JUSTICE FOR LAUGHING BOY

CONNOR SPARROWHAWK –
A DEATH BY INDIFFERENCE

Sara Ryan

Jessica Kingsley *Publishers*
London and Philadelphia

First published in 2018
by Jessica Kingsley Publishers
73 Collier Street
London N1 9BE, UK
and
400 Market Street, Suite 400
Philadelphia, PA 19106, USA

www.jkp.com

Copyright © Sara Ryan 2018

Front cover image source: Sara Ryan.

Library of Congress Cataloging in Publication Data
A CIP catalog record for this book is available from the Library of Congress

British Library Cataloguing in Publication Data
A CIP catalogue record for this book is available from the British Library

ISBN 978 1 78592 348 7
eISBN 978 1 78450 683 4

Printed and bound in Great Britain

Contents

For all the Weary Mothers (and Fathers),
and the nieces and nephews who
will never meet Connor.

Foreword

I always say that the people who taught me about human rights and the law were my clients: people who were wrongly accused of crimes they did not commit; women and children who were not listened to when they had been raped, abused or battered; people who suffered persecution in their homeland but faced a wall of disbelief when they sought asylum here; people who because of their race, sexuality, religion or other difference were subjected to the pain and humiliation of mistreatment; vulnerable people who suffered neglect and cruelty or indifference at the hands of the state. Theirs were stories of deep inhumanity yet securing justice was no mean feat. Institutions close ranks to protect reputations and persons in authority all too often defend the indefensible.

Connor Sparrowhawk was without doubt an extraordinary human being. His learning difficulties and epilepsy may have meant he needed special care but he was a life-loving, talented and amazing boy with a hugely supportive family and a great network of friends. He died by drowning in a shabby, under-resourced NHS unit for those with special needs. He was on his own in a locked bathroom when he had an epileptic seizure; no one was within hearing distance.

Nurses and other carers had not been informed of his medical condition and received no training whatsoever in how to deal with such an event. This is the human cost of austerity policies. I wept when I read this powerful book.

The suffering of families who face tragedy can be unbearable. To their grief is often added the inability or unwillingness of the authorities to explain what happened. When relatives seek explanations, they frequently face obstruction, lies, delaying tactics and non-disclosure of relevant evidence. Then they are the ones accused of being vexatious and trouble making.

Yet in the face of such wrongfulness what always amazes me is that some incredible people find resilience and strength to persist in their quest for justice. These are the true champions of human rights – not lawyers.

Connor's mother Sara Ryan is a remarkable woman. She could not let the death of her son go unquestioned. She could not rest until she had answers and placed responsibility at the doors of those who were really guilty of failing Connor. Those people further up the chain of command who are richly rewarded yet rarely held to account.

Sara took the arduous course of seeking a public inquest into her son's death. She was supported by the wonderful team at INQUEST, a great NGO which seeks open justice for unexplained or preventable deaths. Family, friends and acquaintances built a strong and vibrant campaign around the tragic loss of Connor. And I am proud to say that a group of amazing, committed lawyers from my own chambers argued the case and fought successfully for the family.

Justice involves openness and accountability. Sara's recounting of her family's journey lays bare the deep inequities within our legal system and our society as a whole.

People with learning difficulties and autism receive insufficient support and care. People seeking justice face a system skewered in favour of those with money and resource.

This book is both heart-warming and heart breaking. It is a story of love. The pursuit of justice for Connor was a battle for us all. We cannot remain silent as our welfare state, our health and care system is starved of resource and brought to its knees. We cannot walk on by as the gulf grows between rich and poor. This book is about the society we live in and duty we all have to care for each other.

Baroness Helena Kennedy QC

Author's Note

My name is Sara Ryan and my partner is Richard Huggins. We have five children: Rosie, Will, Connor, Owen and Tom. Richard and I live in an Oxford suburb with Tom, our youngest.

This book tells the story of our family, our son Connor and our fight for justice. It describes real events, but given the number of people who offered their help over the past few years some names have had to be left out to simplify the telling of our story.

Thank you to all those who have offered help and assistance over the years and to those who continue to seek #JusticeforLB.

I died this morning.

In the bath.

I'm dead now.

Mum? Am I dead, Mum?

4 July 2013

That morning. 4 July 2013. I've patchy memories. Some things remain crystal clear. It was baking hot and I caught the bus into Oxford as usual – I work at Oxford University as a researcher.

Fran, a friend who has a son in Connor's class, texted to ask if he was going to go to the school prom the following evening. I replied saying I'd ask him later when I visited him.

He was due to visit the Oxford Bus Company that morning. I didn't (and still don't) remember walking through the market in Gloucester Green on the way to work but later found photos I'd taken. Photos of the remarkably mundane, a sort of final capturing of everyday life in Oxford city centre on a mid-summer Thursday morning. Of life as it was.

I remember I'd bought breakfast or lunch and, unusually for me, put it in the staff fridge in our enormous, open-plan office. I'm not a 'keep-things-chilled' sort of person. Closing the fridge door was the last thing I did before my mobile rang. Dr Jayawant from the Unit. Was it a good time to talk? Connor was on his way to the John Radcliffe Hospital. Found in the bath. Unconscious... Sunshine was spilling into the open-plan space through grubby windows. Very few people around still. I headed out of the office, checking details with her.

Did I use the lift? I must have. I hung up, walked through the glass doors, back out onto the street and was heading to the bus stop before the details began to seep in. Was it a good time to talk...?

Much later, at Connor's inquest, the 999 call that the same consultant psychiatrist made to emergency services was played to the jury. She was so relaxed and unforthcoming;

the responder suggested a four-hour response slot. Back out in brilliant sunshine I realised I should probably get a cab. I rang Caroline, our office administrator, to say I was going to the hospital. She came straight down and caught up with me outside the railway station. Caroline has a learning-disabled daughter in her forties.

Rich, who is also an academic specialising in political science at Oxford Brookes University, was at a staff event in the Town Hall. I texted him and Fran from the cab. Calm texts. Connor was on his way to the John Radcliffe. He'd been there before in an ambulance, after all. I thought about the information I'd been told, in an odd, slightly fragmented way.

Found unconscious in the bath.

Airway cleared before going in the ambulance...

His key nurse was with him and would ring if there was any change...

Any change?

The black cab crawled along the Banbury Road towards the hospital. The sun continued to bake. Each metre covered brought increasingly harrowing, tumbling and terrifying thoughts. My colleague Caroline remained calm. I repeatedly returned to whether Connor was conscious or not and whether he might have experienced some sort of neurological damage. This sent me into a sort of hysteria (in my mind...I don't think I shared it). What if he was in a coma? I kept trying, and failing, to imagine what a brain injury might mean for Connor.

He'd been found unconscious in the bath. What did that mean?

What could that possibly *mean*?

Caroline repeatedly said we just didn't know. It was a journey that defied sense-making.

We pulled up outside the entrance to A&E realising neither of us had any cash. Caroline had left work without her bag. I had some euros from a recent work trip to Finland. I stuffed them into the driver's hand and ran past reception to the ambulance arrival area. A few years earlier I'd beaten the ambulance to the hospital after Connor had a seizure at school. On that occasion, he was wheeled out of the vehicle on a trolley, beaming and basking in the attention from the paramedics, ready to go home after a few hours of checks.

This time my friend Mary was waiting for me – she also has two learning-disabled children and worked on reception in A&E. She had seen Connor's name appear on the system half an hour or so earlier.

Thinking back, I can't imagine what that morning was like for Mary, or for Caroline who travelled with me, or for the serious and sensitive consultant who appeared from nowhere to tell me the bare facts without hesitation.

A ventilator was keeping Connor breathing in a resuscitation room to the left of us. There was nothing that could be done. A moment, a lifetime, of indescribable terror that unfolded in a hideous slow motion.

PART I

CONNOR

CHAPTER 1

What a Wonderful World

When Connor was about four or five, I bought a video camera in time for the extravaganza his school put on each summer. Rosie was allowed to duck out of her primary school to come along and we pitched up to watch the performance called 'Round the World'. Amid the typical cacophony, each school year was led into the hall dressed in traditional clothes from different countries. Connor's class appeared in colourful South American tunics and sombreros and were organised into a jumbled semi-circle with teachers and teaching assistants.

I eventually managed to find Connor through my viewfinder; his angelic and chubby little face a study in bafflement, seriousness and stoicism, and his head half-cocked. I pressed 'record' seconds before they started singing *What a Wonderful World* and managed to capture around ten seconds of Connor and his classmates singing and signing:

I hear babies crying, I watch them grow

They'll learn much more than I'll never know

And I think to myself what a wonderful world

The rest of the footage is a chaotic and inept sweeping of floor, feet and chair legs. At the time, I pegged this as a complete failing on the filming front, those blooming tears interfering with my camera smarts. Now I think the film captured the moment perfectly: brilliance, poignancy, chaos and uncertainty. And staff offering unending support, enthusiasm and encouragement.

At the time, I wrote, 'In this setting, unlike most others, our kids have no limits.'

Connor

Connor is who Connor is, really. A friend who had known  him since he was a baby said that someone recently asked him what Connor was like. He said he couldn't say much other than he's 'just Connor' and that pretty much sums him up. We've been asked to describe him repeatedly over the past few years and come up with these blandish statements about 'quirky', 'funny', 'loving', 'brilliant sense of humour', but these words don't capture the essence of a young man who sat outside definitions of what is considered 'normal' while often exposing them for their oddity. He skirted mainstream life, dipping into the bits he liked, or the bits he was forced to endure because we, school or others made him.

He loved his family, our dog Chunky Stan, sitting in the sunshine, reading *Horrible Histories*, watching YouTube films of lorries loading on and off cross-channel ferries, the Mighty Boosh, septic tanks, Eddie Stobart lorries and London buses.

I used to call him my 'unlikely ethnographer', as his rule-breaking often revealed as much about the banality or stupidity of unwritten social rules as it did about him not doing what he was told. He didn't get involved in the typical bickering and negotiations of childhood. The five kids used to have 50p each to buy sweets every Saturday morning, which could involve some serious, and sometimes heated, negotiations over 'three for £1' sweet deals at the Co-op. Connor unfailingly chose a packet of fruit pastilles every Saturday for about 15 years. He'd ask for one thing for Christmas. This didn't stop us buying him other presents, but that one thing – the Woody from Toy Story outfit, the cattle truck with an opening door, the Routemaster die-cast model – was what he wanted; the rest was white noise.

He had a number of unusual outfits when he was younger. An Early Learning Centre police tabard was worn for a good ten years, often with an orange pair of plastic binoculars and one of a selection of baseball caps. One summer, on holiday in France with wider family, he took to wearing swimming goggles (out of the pool) with one of those plastic shower caps you get free in a hotel. As he grew older, he became more conventional in what he wore, although his collection of baseball caps continued to grow. He grew into a slender and beautiful young man, with a rock-star mop and chiselled cheekbones. His approach to life was one of simplicity, straightforwardness and delight in the things, the people and the dog he loved. He was a cool kid. And we all loved the socks off him.

Sadly, this coolness was overshadowed during his childhood by diagnoses of autism, global developmental delay and various other labels – a relentless focus on deficit. We were sucked into the black hole of disability being a tragedy.

This was never more apparent than when Connor was about two years old and the 'kindly' paediatrician at the John Radcliffe Hospital said there was nothing that could be 'done' and we would probably need to look into some kind of respite as Connor grew older. She could say nothing positive.

An obliteration of a lifetime in a few, thoughtless words leaving me in search of somehow 'curing' Connor. I feel a sad angriness about this now. How can you cure quirkiness? And why would you want to?

I organised months of autism obedience-type lessons known as 'Lovaas' at home, which involved Connor upstairs in his bedroom with a series of teachers (in practice, a handful of students from Oxford Brookes and a well-meaning woman who was evangelical about 'training' autistic kids) being drilled through various, broken-down tasks, tables and tick boxes. He was around three at this stage and his cheeky, cheerful older sister Rosie was thriving at the local primary school across the road from us. I was determined to prise open a space for Connor to get in there somehow, and it wasn't going to happen while he didn't talk and hung out in the kitchen swing bin (with the lid on) whenever it was empty.

Eventually, he started to talk when he was around four, but the mainstream space failed to materialise. The headteacher at Rosie's school could not be clearer about this during the briefest of brief meetings in her lightly hyacinth-scented office, one morning before school started. One of those non-meetings parents of disabled children become all too familiar with.

'Your son? Here? I really don't think so...'

Instead he was collected every morning by local authority transport and taken to the John Watson 'special' school in a village about five miles from where we lived. He was to stay at that school for the rest of his life.

The early years

There were some tough times, particularly before Connor reached secondary school. Epic distress around shops, lighting, sounds and reversing the car. He could be unreachable, inconsolable and remarkably banshee-like when something upset him. At that time, I was doing a sociology and anthropology degree, part time at Oxford Brookes University. Connor was diagnosed soon after I started this and, like other parents of disabled children, I went on to specialise in learning disability, autism and difference. While I was studying, my mum (a retired building society manager), stayed overnight mid-week to help with the kids, as well as providing a magical sprinkling of cleaning and order to our lives.

During this time, the things that too often caused Connor distress were the stuff of everyday life: a bus not running, the car breaking down, a wing mirror or windscreen wiper snapping off a die-cast bus model. Talking through what was going to happen that day, or the following day, while trying to anticipate and feed into the plan any contingencies, was a tricky endeavour too often doomed to failure because of the vagaries of life, or due to us failing to fully understand how to break down activities into digestible chunks.

One example, of so many, took place on a camping trip. Rich often took some of the kids camping at weekends. The first time Connor went, neither of us thought to explain to him that the trip was for two nights. I mean, a camping trip starting on Friday night, 50 or 60 miles away, has got to be two nights. Hasn't it? I got a cheery call from Rich in the New Forest on the Friday evening. The tent was up, the sun was out, they'd been to the beach, eaten fish and chips and everyone was having a ball. I could hear the excited and happy chatter in the background. The next morning, Connor woke and got ready to come home. There was no dissuading him; we hadn't told him it was a two-night trip.

Sleep, or no sleep, was a feature of those early years. Connor, while happy to be in his room at bedtime and throughout the night, didn't sleep much and would often be quite vocal re-living his day. He could mimic voices to perfection and sometimes it sounded as if his whole class and teacher were in his room. It was fascinating and exhausting as he had a knack of absorbing phrases or soundbites he'd heard during the day and weaving them seamlessly into his narrative. In contrast, every so often, he'd come home from school and sleep for hours without stirring.

This unusual pattern confounded a sleep study he was enrolled on at Oxford University when he was around six years old. It was sold to us as a way of helping him learn to sleep better. He had to wear a device round his ankle monitoring his sleep patterns for a week. The researcher came back with a print-out chart showing very little sleep and muttered something about a faulty device. Connor repeated the week, which produced similar results. He was promptly de-enrolled from the study; his sleep patterns would skew the overall results.

'Hey! What do we do about him not sleeping?' I asked, slightly hysterically, as the researcher gathered his consent forms, clunky device and study paperwork and beat a hasty retreat down the garden path.

'Er, have you thought about a star chart?'

The star chart. Christ, I hate star charts. A tyrannical device rewarding 'good' behaviour with stickers with a view to getting a prize after a certain number of star stickers. For kids like Connor, this is about as useful as a fish slice made of Play-doh. The star chart is, really, a red flag signalling the limitations of available support and services. These are typically organised in a rigid and inflexible way, venturing nowhere near the terrain you need to traverse in order to provide effective help or support.

During these early years, my undergraduate study led to a PhD at the University of Warwick, and I'd read an academic article or book chapter in the bath each night before treating myself to the newspaper or a mag. Connor would invariably be up and chatting away to himself in his bedroom. For months he would repeatedly call out:

'Mum? Are you my mum, Mum?'

'Yes.'

'Yes.'

'Yes.'

(Through gritted teeth while reading Erving Goffman's classic book *Stigma*.)

A few years later, I started working at Oxford University as a researcher on a project that involved interviewing autistic adults and parents of autistic children about their experiences. One mother told me her daughter had taken a while to work out categories – like 'mum' and 'pet' – and then to understand who belonged in each category.

I finally realised what Connor was asking me.

'Mum? Are you my "mum", Mum?'

(Yes, matey. I'm your mum and I love you to the moon and back.)

In 2002, when Connor was eight, we moved to our current home – a 1930s semi in an Oxford suburb. The house had been empty for a few years and needed a complete overhaul. Urine-soaked carpets and mouldy curtains, a kitchen with the narrowest of wooden cupboards and an under-stairs larder with stone shelves. That summer, we stripped, painted and sanded. I remember Connor had one of his frequent ear infections and lay outside in the baking sunshine on the yellowing grass in the small, overgrown garden. No moans, groans or whingeing.

Between 2002 and 2008 we got the kitchen extended and the garage transformed into a bedroom and bathroom, with half an eye on Connor's early adulthood. Rich and I used the extension for the time being while the kids were upstairs in various permutations of bedroom-sharing. Tom, the youngest, and Connor shared a typically messy room filled with Lego, Playmobil and Connor's growing collection of die-cast models. Connor was given an Early Learning Centre plastic-coated town map when he was about two and this was spread out on the bedroom floor where he would lie on the floor, lining up buses and moving them slowly and meticulously. It eventually became 'Connortown': the planned location of the haulage company, 'ConnorCo', he dreamed of owning.

Our house is just off the London Road in Oxford – the main road from London into the city centre, with a constant stream of buses: the numbers 2, 2a, 280, 800, U1, 280 and 400 to the city centre, the Oxford Tube and X90 to and from London, the National Express to Stansted and Airline services to Heathrow and Gatwick. Connor frequently stood, looking out of his bedroom window, absorbed in watching the passing vehicles.

Summers passed. The school bus pitched up during term time. Special school became an established part of Connor's and our lives.

The blog

I began writing a blog called mydaftlife (https://mydaftlife. com) in 2011 when Connor was 15. This was mostly to document the funny stories that happened in our everyday lives. It began as a random combination of observations of life: mealtimes, days out, holidays and some travelling adventures and mishaps, illustrated with photos from my ever-ready and always-snapping camera.

The first story I wrote was one that makes me chuckle still when I think about it. Connor was around seven or eight and was off school with some sort of light-touch illness that meant a pyjama day on the settee, snoozing in front of a video of *Barney and Friends* on (repeated) repeat. Late morning, I realised we were out of milk and, after some deliberation (we live about 50 metres from the Co-op), I decided to risk leaving Connor home alone and leg it to the supermarket.

I spent about 15 minutes carefully explaining what I was going to do and how he wasn't, under any circumstances, to move from the settee. I rehearsed and re-rehearsed every scenario I could think of to make sure he fully understood that, no matter what, he was to stay put; even if the postman knocked or a parcel was delivered, a friend called round, he thought he heard a noise, Chunky Stan wanted to go out in the back garden, he was to stay put. He was to stay put on the settee watching his beloved Barney. I would be gone for minutes.

I grabbed my purse and left the house realising the second I pulled the front door shut, I'd forgotten my key. Fear and hysterical laughter...I started to try and communicate with Connor through the window.

'You know everything I just told you? Forget it! It's your mum, Connor!'

He resolutely and steadfastly ignored me. Eventually, with much coaxing (and believe me, it was a lot of coaxing), Connor edged off the sofa and half opened the window enough for me to pull it open and clamber back in. All the while he never once took his eyes off that singing, purple dinosaur.

It wasn't long before my blog developed a readership beyond immediate family and friends, much to my surprise. It was written anonymously (Connor was 'Laughing Boy' or 'LB' for short) with no identifiable location, but it generated interest; and my reasonably regular rehashing of what was often funny mealtime banter, or other, everyday exchanges, seemed to resonate with people.

Many of the posts were simply a few lines reporting a snippet of daily life. Connor had a school diary in which his teachers wrote a paragraph about his day, and I'd often ask him to elaborate on these. This, from October 2011, is just one example:

'Hey LB! How did meal prep go today?'

'Not good, Mum.'

'Oh. Why not?'

'I failed, Mum.'

'Whaddayamean, you failed?'

'I failed, Mum.'

'Why? What did you cook?'

'Kebabs, Mum.'

'Oh. I don't get it. What went wrong?'

'I didn't have a skewer, Mum.'

'Oh. Why not?'

'Dunno, Mum.'

'So what did you eat for lunch?'

'Bits, Mum.'

It was an irreverent, spontaneous, snapshot of family life where things were less than straightforward, with a good dose of humour and swear words.

I love lorries, Connor. And buses and coaches...

Do you love lorries, Mum?

Yes.

Mum?

Do you love lorries, Mum?

Yes. I do. I look out for them all the time. Wherever I am.

Why, Mum?

Because you did.

Mum, I love lorries, Mum.

I know Connor.

How do you know, Mum?

Because you told me.

Did I tell you, Mum?

Yep. All the time.

CHAPTER 2

Dog Days, Holidays and Life Rafts

Holidays were always a bit of an adventure, at best. Not least because of the inevitable disruption to predictable, daily routines and the level of planning that needed to be carried out beforehand and throughout. It's probably fair to say we had a spiky holiday profile, factoring in the British weather, the octopus-like herding skills necessary for chasing around five lively kids, and random events like a cheerful driver very gently ramming into us at a roundabout in the Lake District, leaving the boot out of action, and a long journey home with belongings piled high on our laps.

When Connor was about eight we had two consecutive holidays renting a cottage in Kirby Lonsdale, straddling the border of Lancashire and Yorkshire. It was a spectacularly located house, hidden away on the bank of the river Lune, which could be reached by a very steep, short road from the town centre. We hung out by the riverside under a tree canopy, with the kids paddling and building dams, had barbecues of an evening, and Chunky Stan pretending not to see the giant rabbits that faced him in the garden each morning. One day, after flicking through the bulging set of leaflets in the information folder in the cottage, we decided to visit White Scar Cave, a nearby tourist attraction.

We turned up, bought tickets, the kids were given hard hats and we waited to be guided through the cave. I later wrote about the tour on my blog:

We went to White Scar show cave once. Britain's longest show cave, one mile underground. We put on our helmets (LB loves anything to do with emergency services) and set off in a party of about 20. Our guide, a white-haired cave enthusiast, led us along the narrow passages until we reached the highlight of tour, Battlefield Cavern. It was spectacular. The guide asked Rich to turn the light off as he was standing by the switch. There was a collective 'Aaaahhhhh…' as we stood on a wooden platform marvelling the glowing stalagmites and stalactites. But switching off the lights was not a good idea.

LB started to quietly pray. Eh?

'Dear God, please get me out of this cave safely…'

We all looked at each other. A few people turned round to look at him.

'Dear God. GET ME OUT. GOD! HELP ME…'

'Shh…LB. Shhhh now. Don't be silly…'

'Shhhhhhh LB…' hissed the kids, nudging him.

'God. Johnny English. Dear Johnny English save me, Johnny English…'

'Shhhhhhhhhhhhhhhhhhh…'

'…save me from the cave. Johnny English. HELP US. THE ROOF IS GOING TO FALL IN. WE. ARE. ALL. GOING. TO. DIE!!!'

Oh crap. Crap. Crap. Crap. Things disintegrated pretty quickly at that point. Britain's longest show cave and all that. A mile underground. 'Turn the light back on!' shouted the guide, as Rich scrabbled round trying to find the switch. Children started crying, parents got agitated, LB kept praying. Loudly.

It's probably fair to say we got out of the cave in record speed. A cross between a fast walk and a jog. Parties coming the other way were forced against the wall, as the guide, followed very closely by LB (still calling for Johnny English), went into emergency exit overdrive.

Eventually we saw daylight. LB stopped praying and cheered up.

'Funny little lad,' said the guide, panting, 'is he all right?'

There were complicated layers going on that day, and it was a familiar pattern.

Connor was scared, and his distress could be intense and unwieldy, demanding complete attention. His distress, and the obvious discomfort or disruption it could cause others, could upset the rest of the kids. Rich and I would be upset that one, some or all of the kids were upset, or that other people had responded inappropriately.

As a bit of an aside, instead of tutting, staring or glaring at what you might think is the behaviour of a naughty or spoiled child, it would ease the lives of families enormously if you could simply ignore the minor disruption to your life, or just smile.

As the years passed, the responses of unknown others became less stinging and pretty much faded into irrelevance. Regular disruptions in public spaces became so commonplace that they evolved into a source of fascination and occasional amusement. These experiences led to my PhD focus on mothers' experiences of going out in public with their 'busy' children.

In 2011, when Connor was 15, we rented two yurts on a North Devon farm. A breathtaking setting and, for once, the weather was sunny and warm. The first couple of days were a bit tense as Connor became convinced the farmer was on Interpol's most wanted criminal list. He repeatedly raged and gesticulated at him from a distance, in between staring intently at the ground, hands thrust into his pockets, muttering about the need to catch this master criminal. You had to hand it to him, he was nothing if not dogged when he believed a crime or some wrongdoing had been committed. As it was, the farmer somehow allayed Connor's concerns and they ended up collecting eggs together in a companionable silence.

On most days, Rich, Owen and Tom would go off fishing while Connor and I hung out on the farm. Once the Interpol issue was resolved, Connor found contentment in the space like he did at home. He spent a lot of time with three bullocks, which Rich referred to in his talk at Connor's funeral:

'Gentle and compassionate, his innate understanding of the way things would be was imparted in quiet chunks of insight, determined questioning and, at times, reassuring homilies. One holiday in Devon he spent many hours talking to three *fine Aberdeen Angus bullocks who faced their last days before slaughter in a nearby barn on the campsite. Touched by their plight, Connor sought to reassure them that despite the inevitability of their impending doom, they would feel little or no pain, that they were headed for better things and, as this was their destiny, they should embrace it and not worry or be distressed. When asked where this "better place" might be, he replied the supermarket and dinner plate; his compassion real but also realistic.'*

The epilepsy

Epilepsy crept into our lives with some stealth, brief absences and disappearings. Small signs were missed, but picked up retrospectively, such as an incident when Connor was about five, described by the GP as a 'febrile seizure'. There were odd moments of distraction. It was only when Connor was 15 and we were watching the film *UP*, with the kids squidged together on the settee, that the penny dropped. Connor became so distressed about the danger to the grandad that he fleetingly lost consciousness.

A terrible penny – a friend who was researching experiences of epilepsy had recently interviewed a couple of parents whose children had died of SUDEP (sudden unexplained death in epilepsy). This is a contested diagnosis because it tends to happen when the person is alone. A sadness and low-level fear entered our lives at that point.

Getting a diagnosis of epilepsy was a familiar battle as we were batted back from paediatric neurology with the 'just a bit of anxiety, perhaps try a star chart' offering.

A few days later, I had a call at work from Connor's deputy headteacher:

'He's absolutely fine, but Connor is with the paramedics. We think he had a tonic-clonic seizure.[1] He's regained consciousness but is going to be taken to the John Radcliffe just to be checked over...'

That was the time I ran from work to the hospital and beat the ambulance (our office was about a ten-minute walk from the hospital). Relief washed over me when Connor appeared, unharmed. From top of the, until then unknown, fear scale to overwhelming love for this funny boy who shouldn't have to deal with the additional challenges of a neurological disorder.

The next morning, I rang the GP to ask for a re-referral to neurology. This was bounced back because Connor had by then entered adult services, aged 16. There was a referral to adult neurology, and two or three more tonic-clonic seizures and paramedic outings, before he was finally diagnosed with epilepsy. It was a mountain climb to diagnosis that I suspect most mainstream kids are not forced to endure.

I felt inordinately sad when I later found out he was never invited to the 'First Fit' Clinic, an introductory clinic for newly diagnosed patients. The exclusionary roots run so blinking deep.

The difficulties we experienced getting treatment for Connor's health needs reflect the difficulties that many learning-disabled people experience. I'm convinced autism and learning disability labels eclipse engagement with actual health issues, and this contributes to the well-documented premature mortality of learning-disabled people in the UK.

---

1   Tonic-clonic seizures or convulsions, which used to be known as 'grand mal', involve a stiffening of the body and then convulsions and a loss of consciousness.

The confidential inquiry into the premature deaths of people with learning disabilities (CIPOLD), published in 2013, found that learning-disabled women die, on average, 20 years earlier, and learning-disabled men 13 years earlier, than women and men in the general population.[2]

These labels are experienced in different ways, at different times, in different contexts. Rosie, for example, was very much part of Connor's diagnostic process as she was used as a comparator, while Tom found out that Connor was autistic when he was at a friend's house watching the television and the friend's dad mentioned that Connor was autistic. Another friend said he only realised once Connor died. These labels often have more currency outside the family where they are a necessary device for trying to get appropriate support.

In effect, people who are given these labels are not valued or treated as fully human. While we might kid ourselves that progress has been made, the way in which health services are organised and professionals trained still overwhelmingly favours a 'medical model' of learning disability or autism while, ironically or otherwise, missing health symptoms and diagnoses.

Attitudes towards learning-disabled people in particular are entrenched and pervasive. Fears around the 'feeble minded' diluting the strength of national stock were at their height in the pre-war years with respected 'intellectual elites', including George Bernard Shaw, William Beveridge

---

2   Heslop, P., Blair, P., Fleming, P., Hoghton, M. *et al.* (2013) *The confidential inquiry into premature deaths of people with learning disabilities (CIPOLD).* Final report, Executive Summary, Easy read report, and Easy read summary report. Bristol, UK, University of Bristol.

and Marie Stopes, arguing for the reduction or removal of 'defectives'.[3]

While eugenics was discredited after World War Two, the stain remains, and perceptions of learning-disabled people as weak and somehow to be reviled are, arguably, reflected both in the premature mortality rates and levels of hate crime in the UK[4] as well as the general level of lukewarm outrage demonstrated by the British public to documented experiences of abuse. While there was an enormous outcry in response to the screening of the *Panorama* Winterbourne View documentary in 2011, in March 2017, a Channel 4 *Dispatches* programme, 'Under Lock and Key', which revealed similar levels of abuse, barely generated any interest.

Connor hated the diagnosis of epilepsy. When he snouted out the word 'autism' in a school letter some years earlier and asked about it, we explained that everyone had something, whether they knew it yet or not. He ran with this and would often ask what someone 'had'. I remember picking him up from after-school club with Radio Two playing in the car. Connor found the DJ Simon Mayo deeply boring (sorry Simon). He'd either mutter about Simon Mayo being sacked, or ask endless questions about Steve Wright, who he loved: *'Where was Steve Wright born, Mum?' 'Is Steve Wright a Londoner, Mum?' 'Mum, do you like Steve Wright, Mum?'* One day he asked, *'What has Steve Wright got, Mum?'*

'DJitis,' I said, grimly navigating the Green Road roundabout. We had a good old chuckle at this.

---

3   https://www.theguardian.com/commentisfree/2012/feb/17/eugenics-skeleton-rattles-loudest-closet-left

4   See K. Quarmby, *Scapegoat: Why We are Failing Disabled People* (Portobello, 2011), for further analysis.

Connor seemed to understand and accept he was autistic but I suspect that, just like we had failed to specify two nights on the camping trip, or to understand the 'mum' questions, we'd closed down a space for him in those early discussions to understand that some people may have more than one label or diagnosis. It simply didn't cross our minds.

While he refused to engage with the idea of epilepsy, he took his daily medication – one tablet of phenytoin every morning – without question. And, from when he was eventually diagnosed in 2011 aged 16, up to January 2013, aged 18, when the GP prescribed him an anti-depressant to try to help his mood, his seizures were under control.

Chunky Stan, 2003–16

Stan became part of our family in June 2003. A Jack Russell puppy I collected with the kids to surprise Rich for his 40th birthday. We'd had numerous conversations about getting a dog, which, given the general state of chaos and disorganisation in our home, was a stretch. We had a 'melded' family with Rich's boys from his previous relationship, Will and Owen, coming each weekend and on holidays, Rosie and Connor staying with their dad at weekends and holidays, and Tom, who memorably announced one weekend that he was going to stay with his 'other-dad-called-Ned-Flanders-who-lives-on-a-farm' (all in one breath), stuck with us.

Rich maintains we never agreed to a dog and he's always hated Jack Russell terriers.

I can't describe the excitement of that trip, but you can probably imagine: young kids and the cutest puppy imaginable. Rich opened the front door, took one look at the pup we were cradling like some sort of long-lost treasure and thundered:

> *'If that's a Jack Russell puppy you can take it straight out of here...'*

From sparkle to snarkle in less than 20 seconds.

Luckily, he recovered his equilibrium pretty much immediately and Stan became a central family member. He was a classic chunky, light brown and white Jack Russell who excelled in dribbling a football and loved being fussed over. A photo of his legs and paws, next to Tom's feet, features in the design of my blog.

Connor in particular developed a close relationship with Stan that was in part grotesque and part practical. Each morning Connor would look out of the window for the school bus, with Stan maintaining vigil with him on the windowsill. Connor talked to Stan a lot, in a high-pitched voice. We realised that, while Connor would often ignore questions we asked him, if we said Stan wanted to know Connor would provide elaborate detail about what he'd been doing or what he thought about something. The less positive part to their relationship was the tendency for Connor to let, or encourage, Stan to slobber all over his face and mouth.

When Connor was about 15, Stan developed glaucoma and had one eye removed. Nearly a year after Connor died, in May 2014, Stan's other eye went and the vet – a brusque, Scottish eye specialist – explained that it was unlikely Stan would cope well with no sight. He could remove the second eye and see how he responded but there was a good chance he should be put down. Going back to the surgery the next day, I was surprised to see a slightly stumbling Stan being walked in the sunny garden through the reception window. A few minutes later, the vet walked into the waiting room beaming and holding Stan, tail wagging, in his arms.

He was eventually put down two years later. We scattered his ashes on Connor's woodland grave, killing the grass for a few months.

Negotiating mediocrity and the life raft

A general short-changing of life comes with the territory once you are diagnosed with a learning disability in the UK. Opportunities are closed off and mediocrity becomes the norm, or even considered as good. Families, particularly mothers, are expected to perform a range of tasks over and above typical parenting stuff with the spectre of the 'lack of resources' stick waiting in the wings to bat away the outrageous mother who dares to question the breadcrumbs thrown at her child or children.

However, we found pockets of brilliance amidst the mediocrity, where there is sunshine, fun and genuine support. Small charities like Parasol (www.parasolproject.org), which runs inclusive activities, and a student-run sports club called KEEN – Kids Enjoy Exercise Now (www.keenoxford.org), both based in Oxford, really stood out for our family. Then there are the well-meaning but poorly thought-through 'performed' special needs circuses that involve some sort of payback, like being forced to wear a t-shirt publicising the charity or the organisation providing the 'treat' – in effect singling out the kids and their families as 'special'.

Having a good bunch of mates with kids in Connor's school meant we were able to have a chuckle at, and rage about, this degrading nonsense over the years, while trying to champion the good stuff. With no school gate to meet at, we'd hook up three or four times a year, nosh on cheese until we got the cheese sweats and drink bottle after bottle of prosecco. After our various life-changing experiences, these evenings became nicknamed 'the life raft'.

Connor liked the everyday stuff: the stuff that didn't involve 'disability' and was just about life. After being chucked out of our dental surgery for biting the dentist's finger when she tried to X-ray his teeth, he had a stint at a 'special' dentist in East Oxford for a few appointments, before enough time had passed that we thought we could smuggle him back to the Oxford Brookes surgery. He was assigned a new, young and enthusiastic dentist called Dan.

Connor totally engaged with Dan. He looked forward to appointments, obviously felt comfortable with him and enjoyed the interactions over his teeth. We had numerous conversations about Dan, usually at weekends, thinking about his life and what Dan might be doing that day: in a relationship, enjoying outdoor sports, living in Eynsham. Connor never tired of hearing the details. I don't know why Connor felt so comfortable with Dan. I never asked and, without thinking about it, didn't realise I wouldn't have the chance to ask. It was a rare and welcomed example of life as it should be.

It was also during this time that Connor started the 'Just you and me, Mum' birthday trips to London. This was after Connor's 14th birthday trip to the Tower of London. We managed to miss the Lord Mayor's Parade confounder that probably flashed up on the motorway signs during the Oxford Tube coach journey to London.

After a brief pit stop in a cafe near Marble Arch, we were astonished when a vintage Routemaster bus turned up, complete with conductor, on our route to the Tower of London.

'Blimey. They must have heard it was your birthday, Connor!'

Two stops later, along Oxford Street, the bus completed its journey and we were chucked off to wait for the next one. We then spent hours at the back of an almost static, fully steamed-up bus with some street pastors from Birmingham. Rich would rub the steam off the window with his arm every so often to say that, yes, we were, once again, circulating the Aldwych.

Tom mentioned this trip in a blog post he wrote about Connor on 3 July 2014:

London was by far his favourite place on Earth. He loved it, I think it was the transport system to be honest, the idea of a city with a bus going pretty much everywhere was his dream place. One birthday of his we went to the Tower of London, his love of history and London combined, what could go wrong. Well, apart from the fact we never actually got in, huge amounts of traffic meant that after six or so hours on buses, when we finally arrived at the Tower of London it was closed. All us kids were so annoyed about 'all that travel for nothing!' It was Connor my parents were worried about though. How would he react to the fact we weren't actually going to the Tower? He did not care one bit, he spent the whole day in London on buses, a perfect day for him. That's one of the amazing things about Connor, he is so easy to please and enjoys such small things, and it really is amazing.

'Just you and me, Mum.'

The new-style birthday trips went something like this: first stop the model shop in Holborn where Connor would carefully study the glass cabinets filled with models and eventually choose a limited-edition die-cast coach or bus. Once we'd paid, he'd stand by the cash desk, open the packaging, chuck away the limited-edition certificate and plastic box, and carefully snap off the wing mirrors and windscreen wipers. He'd leave the shop happy while staff stood looking pale, clammy and slightly dazed. I think he'd learned after years of intense distress, when these snapped off within days, to manage the inevitable.

We would then walk, or catch the tube, to Chinatown for lunch where we sat mostly in silence. Connor would tuck into the crispy duck and guzzle his Coke, with his Horse Show of the Year programme and new vehicle carefully placed on the table.

One year he wanted do a bus tour of London. We grabbed some lunch each from the Selfridges food hall – me, stupidly a salad, and Connor a pasty and Coke – and sat upstairs on the open-air bus. It was November and, despite being a sunny day, once the sun dipped down behind the buildings early afternoon (in the City by that point) it was piercingly cold. Connor didn't want to get off at any stop, or do the boat trip included in the ticket price; he wanted to complete the route. There were very few people on the top deck but the guide cheerfully belted out his commentary with some funny jokes and interesting facts. Who knew Sean Connery and Roger Moore lived in the same central London square?

Connor resolutely stared out to the right of the bus paying no attention to requests to look left, right up or down at various sites. At first, I tried to compensate for the poor audience the guide had by looking, nodding and chuckling, but by early afternoon it was so blooming cold I just huddled further against Connor's skinny frame trying to get some warmth.

We arrived back at Marble Arch in the dark, where we'd started hours before, and caught the Oxford Tube home. I don't think I thawed out until we reached the Thornhill Park and Ride, just outside Oxford.

Mum, is Chunky Stan dead, Mum?

Yes, he died after Christmas.

Why, Mum?

He was very old and the vet put him down.

Did the vet put him down, Mum?

Yes.

Why, Mum?

Because he was very uncomfortable and she thought it was kinder. We agreed.

Why, Mum?

Because he was so old.

Mum, am I dead, Mum?

Yes.

Am I old, Mum?

No.

Why, Mum?

You were never allowed the chance to grow old, matey.

CHAPTER 3

Nudging Adulthood

The halcyon years

The secondary school years coincided with Connor easing into life and finding ways of largely managing things that generated distress and anxiety. He developed a contentedness around inhabiting home spaces, helped by our loosening of the reins of what was expected and acceptable behaviour. It was during this period we started referring to Connor as a 'dude'. Without giving it much thought, this seemed to fit with his love of David Bowie and captured his cool character.[1]

He would spend hours in his room re-organising 'Connortown', or the scrap metal depot he began to craft out of his by then enormous collection of die-cast models, lying on the floor or his bed, carefully moving trucks, emergency vehicles, cranes, buses and bus stops. He was utterly engrossed and chattering away to himself. The staff from the model shop would have got paler and clammier

---

[1]   Later, during our campaign for justice for Connor, use of the term 'dude' spread and some self-advocates began using the term to describe themselves. There was some discussion around it being a conventionally male term and, on Facebook and Twitter discussions, some people talked about 'dudes' and 'dudettes'.

if they'd seen the way he would carefully lift up buses and lorries and drop them in a 'scrap metal' pile.

When a football match was on (and with Rich, Will, Owen and Tom all avid footy fans, this was often), Connor would bring down his box of 'football guys' (the plastic figures you buy in packs with large heads and flat bases) and the football made of scrunched paper and sticky tape made by one of the kids when his tiny toy ball disappeared. He would lie on the wooden floor recreating a match which bore no resemblance to the match being played or conventional football. He attended football club after school each week, seemingly unconcerned when, in goal, he let in 'a thousand goals, Mum'. We recently found out he would stand in goal and, when the ball got close, walk away.

When the sun was out, Connor would take a map of the underground or some other treasure – a *Horrible Histories* book, first-aid manual, bus timetable or copy of the *Yellow Pages* – and bask in the garden on a blanket. I would look at him sometimes, remembering the young boy who lay on the sun-baked grass the summer we moved in, and feel proud of the interesting and quirky young man he'd grown into.

Inevitably, during these lengthy periods of absorption one or other of us would butt in and interrupt him. The other kids would variously banter, try to distract him or tempt him to join one or more of them in hanging out with them.

'Hey, Connor! Do you want to make some bus tickets?'

'Bus tickets?'

'Yes, bus tickets. For your bus company.'

'Yes, Owen…'

These interruptions were met with a mix of delight, good humour, mild exasperation and occasionally irritation, quickly doused as they got on so well.

Rosie and Connor had a particularly strong relationship and she intuitively knew how to make him laugh and generally boss him around. From a young age, she acted as best friend and protector. A sister with the fiercest love.

The lack of an imagined future

One of the main things that struck us when Connor approached 18 was the lack of aspiration attached to his future, particularly by social services.

This was underlined during my first meeting with his care manager. Connor had gone to school not best pleased after I told him she would be coming to school later that morning. She came round to meet me first, with his children's social worker. It was not a good start.

'Would you like tea or coffee?'

'Tea, please. By the way, I won't be able to go to school this morning to meet Connor. I have to be somewhere else.'

'Ah,' I said cheerfully, filling the kettle, 'no worries, he wasn't keen on meeting you.'

'Well,' she said, with a deep sniff, 'I am his future.'

[Frozen pause.]

Connor himself had ambitious plans. He wanted to own his own haulage company and marry a beautiful, brown-eyed woman. He would apply himself to particular tasks diligently and with commitment. He had been a valued caretaker's assistant at school where he excelled in litter picking, a task which fed into his interest in recycling.

Unfortunately, employment wasn't a word that social care used in the few meetings we had during Connor's 'transition'. Given only 6 per cent of learning-disabled adults[2] and 16 per cent of autistic adults[3] are in employment in the UK, this should be a key focus of services and support but 'indicative budgets' and the 'panel' dominate social care discussion. It's a resource-driven approach that strips away any humanity and any imagined future. In my view, Connor and his peers were treated as troublesome and costly bundles in a way that reminded me of the paediatrician talking about respite, back when he was a tot.

In stark contrast, my friend Fran arranged for Connor to be interviewed for a volunteer assistant grounds person at Helen House Hospice in February 2013. This children's hospice is in an old convent building, surrounded by beautiful grounds, behind a brick wall, off the Cowley Road. Connor, off school at the time, dressed smartish and we caught the bus there. Waiting in reception to be taken to the interview we saw another young man pitch up and set off to find a wheelbarrow. The receptionist told us he'd worked there for a few years and was going to do a qualification in grounds keeping.

---

2   https://www.mentalhealth.org.uk/learning-disabilities/help-information/statistics/learning-disability-statistics-/187693

3   www.autism.org.uk/get-involved/media-centre/news/2016-10-27-employment-gap.aspx

I later wrote in my blog:

*LB handled the interview the way he largely handles life;
quietly chattering to himself and occasionally breaking off,
when gently encouraged (nagged), to answer. The volunteer
co-ordinator who interviewed him was exceptional. As were
the receptionist and the estate manager who will be in charge
of him. It was one of those very rare times, outside family,
school and some specialist support, that everyday rules are
adjusted (or ditched) to enable a different engagement. One in
which unusual behaviours aren't 'wrong'. Just different.*

    And LB? He rocked it.

He got the job but was admitted to the Unit a month later,
before the required paperwork around risk assessments and
epilepsy was complete.

A taste of the future

By the time Connor was 16, Rosie and Will had left school and
it was mainly Tom and Connor at home. One early evening,
Rich and Connor met me from work and we wandered along
to a Chinese restaurant around the corner. Rich and I had
reflected, on and off, how this would become an increasingly
common experience for the three of us.

While the other kids grew more independent and
developed their own lives, the outlook for Connor remained
limited. He didn't have friends to hang out with, and really,
apart from activities arranged by school, his peer social life
revolved around his brothers and sister and their friends.

We were looking at the menu when Connor said:

'Mum? How was work, Mum?'

It was the first time he'd asked me anything like that, which was pretty cool, underlining how he could do the 'ordinary' stuff as well as the extraordinary. We'd not been to the restaurant before, but Connor managed, as he so often did, to order the best-looking dish off the menu. On another occasion, during a meal at our favourite restaurant, the Aziz, on the Cowley Road, Rich looked on with envy at the dish placed in front of Connor which looked so much better than his chicken tikka masala.

A few weeks later we were ordering a takeaway and Rich said to Connor, *'What did you order at the Aziz last time, Connor? That lamb dish?'*

Without hesitation, he replied, *'Lamborghini.'*

Another comedy genius moment we now treasure beyond words.

Around this time, we were to go to the cinema for the last time with Connor, to see *Skyfall*. Tom later remarked on how Connor had used the light from the terrorist scenes on the London underground to read his bus ticket. This was surprising because he usually enjoyed a bit of a blockbuster. I wonder now if he was demonstrating another way of dealing with the bits of life, or fictional representations of life, he found upsetting.

His beloved London was under terrorist attack and two James Bonds had lived in the same London square.

The downturn

Returning to school after the summer holidays in September 2012, Connor became uncharacteristically unhappy and anxious. In mid-December Rich drove to Devon to bring him home from a school residential trip after he had been threatening a teaching assistant. Connor was convinced this young man had stolen his toolkit. He was unrecognisable and unreachable, repeatedly tugging on a piece of hair, muttering obscenities and lashing out on the journey back.

Instead of mealtimes, holidays and dentist trips, I began documenting on the blog our experiences of trying and failing to get effective support. It became an account of the dismal state of care and support for learning-disabled adults in the UK. This was unfolding under an uneasy coalition government, dominated by the Conservatives and their assertion that it was necessary to impose austerity on Britain. Not only were health and social care under enormous pressure, but learning-disabled people seemed to be very much near the bottom of, or at the bottom of, the support pile.

Things came to a head in March 2013. Between January and early March, Connor was often off school in a state of agitation and unpredictability. At six-feet tall, he had gone from being someone who would dissolve into silent laughter at any attempt to play fight with him, to someone with surprising strength and accuracy. We were too nervous to leave him with people who would usually support him because of this unpredictability and aggression. Rich and I took it in turns to work at home while Connor would, typically, spend days tinkering in the downstairs toilet with his toolkit, muttering to himself or shouting angrily.

On Friday 15 March, there was another call from school. Connor had punched his beloved support teacher, Big Sue, in the face. She was OK but had gone home with a badly bruised jaw. Rich picked up Connor while I phoned the crisis number I'd been given by the care manager. She was off sick or on holiday. I can't remember which, as they seemed to blur into one long absence. When I eventually got through to the duty consultant psychiatrist, he told us to phone the on-call GP if necessary over the weekend. There was nothing he could do because Connor wasn't his patient.

Almost gnawing on the phone in despair, I tried to explain it was not possible to ask Connor to park his intense rage and distress while we rang an on-call GP. He also wasn't anyone's patient; he'd met the community psychiatrist once, very briefly, and she'd discharged him weeks earlier. In the end, I hung up. The consultant rang straight back and said he'd arrange for a prescription of Lorazepam, a sedative, to be picked up from our GP surgery that afternoon.

After a weekend of Connor largely sleeping, I naively assumed the social care cavalry would be on their way first thing Monday morning. We were officially 'in crisis'. There was a real danger that Connor would hurt someone, or himself, badly, and I was terrified he'd end up in the criminal justice system.[4]

Not a dicky bird. I waited until mid-morning and rang the crisis line again. After some confusion because the record of the Friday afternoon exchange was missing, I was told that Connor's psychiatrist – the one who had seen and discharged him – would call me back later that morning. I started to ring through the photocopied list of support services the care manager had given me. By number four, I gave up. Each person who eventually answered the phone was incredulous that a member of the public was ringing, since they were only commissioned by social care.

---

4   An estimated 20–30 per cent of the UK prison population have learning
    disabilities: www.prisonreformtrust.org.uk/Portals/0/Documents/
    Bromley%20Briefings/Summer%202017%20Factfile.pdf

The following day, Tuesday 19 March, my friend Fran rang to say she'd found out that there was a specialist learning disability Short Term Assessment and Treatment Unit, abbreviated as 'STATT', run by Southern Health NHS Foundation Trust and on the Slade House site, just a mile or two from where we lived. There, a team of specialist staff, including psychiatrists, occupational therapists, psychologists and specialist nurses, would be able to observe and assess Connor over the period of a few weeks in order to work out why he was so distressed and unpredictable. He would also be supported to attend school while the assessment was taking place.

The Slade House site. Though we'd met the community psychiatrist for that brief appointment in January 2013, and Connor had attended various psychiatric appointments there over the years, we had no idea that the Assessment and Treatment Unit existed and it was an extraordinary revelation. Fran had been given a phone number I could ring to see if Connor should be admitted. I rang the number, shaking. Connor had been taken out for a brief trip into town that morning by two teaching assistants from school who knew him well (their commitment to Connor, their willingness to bend the rules – Connor was still suspended – and their upset at his uncharacteristic distress and agitation were simply extraordinary). They brought him back early because he was agitated, unpredictable and clearly unwell. Even so, I felt as if a block of ice was lodged in my chest. Phoning that number shrieked against every mothering instinct I had.

Within a few hours of making the call, an on-call psychiatrist, Dr Johnson, came round, spent a short time talking to Connor and then, longer, to us. After making a phone call, he said Connor should be admitted to the Unit that evening and would be 'clerked in' around 8pm. I packed a few things for him and Rich dropped Tom off at judo. He was to walk to his grandparent's house after his judo grading and wait for us.

Connor was OK about going in the car to hospital. He'd enjoyed visiting his grandad some weeks earlier after an accident involving a ladder and some guttering, and he'd always found nurses and paramedics reassuring. However, once we turned left at the crossroads instead of right towards the John Radcliffe, his anxiety increased.

We turned up, in the dark, at a shabby building on the Slade House site and were eventually let in by staff who clearly weren't expecting us, and weren't best pleased to see us. We were told to wait in the living space, a large room with some old sofas and a television screen in a protected plastic casing, while they went to get confirmation Connor was allowed to be admitted that night.

We left, an hour or so later.

In the early hours of that morning, Connor was restrained after he lunged at a support worker. He was pinned face down to the floor by four staff, and sectioned under the Mental Health Act.

That was the day he stopped being a sixth-former.

Opening up the blog

During this time, I had been continuing to blog on mydaftlife.com as life became increasingly difficult, and it had attracted a number of regular commentators, including mothers who had been caring for their children for decades.

They enriched the blog, added their experiences and further underlined the paucity of effective support for people with additional needs. In the space opened up by the blog there was also a growing network of tweeters who included parents, advocacy groups, academics and professionals. They shared experiences and information, and provided critical scrutiny of current policies or other developments. These loose and informal exchanges involved anger at the lack of support, despair at the lack of effective change, and occasional humour.

I began to use the blog to document Connor's time in the Unit. During this time, it became apparent to us that, despite the specialist staff and almost one-to-one support for the five patients (at a cost of £3500 per week per patient), there was little assessment or treatment. Every Monday (except bank holidays, of which there were a few over that period) a meeting was held to discuss each patient in a ten-minute slot. This was typically attended by the psychiatrists, Unit manager and various other staff members. Over the weeks, other than prescribing Connor with Risperidone to calm his distress, I saw little or no assessment or treatment.

We visited daily. Typically, it was me or Rich if we couldn't both make it, the older kids when they were home, my parents, family, friends and school staff. Tom was not allowed to visit because at that point he was 13. There was some talk of Tom and Chunky Stan being allowed to visit the grounds when the weather got better, but when spring arrived we were told this was no longer possible. A meeting was eventually arranged for Connor and Tom at a nearby Burger King. They had not seen each other for a month by this point.

Tom and I pitched up early with a DVD Tom chose for Connor from Tesco and waited. And waited. I rang the Unit.

'Hi. It's Sara. Connor's mum.'

'Hi.'

'Tom and I are at Burger King. You were going to bring Connor to meet us at 6?'

'Oh. Can you hang on while I check the board?'

[Pause]

'Ah, sorry. We forgot. He's just finished eating his tea.'

Choice and hindsight

Once he was admitted to the Unit, the fact that Connor was 18 and an adult meant he was allowed to do what he wanted, with constraints. Well, other than come home, which is all he wanted.

He could choose to stay in his room all day. He could choose to not eat and end up severely underweight (after two months he had a Body Mass Index (BMI) of just 15). We were told we had to phone the Unit each day to ask for Connor's permission to visit, despite set visiting hours being advertised on the door. When I was first told this three days after Connor was admitted and then sectioned for 28 days, I was chilled to the core. What if he said 'No' or, even more concerning, what if the staff said he said 'No'? Just days before, Connor had been at home with his family; now he was sectioned, he'd been brutally restrained and he was at the mercy of people we'd never met before, a few of whom I would never want to meet again.

Even with a 'Yes' to the visiting question, we could not always gain access as the Unit door was not always answered, particularly at weekends or bank holidays. The fakery of 'choice' is, of course, laid bare by such non-answering. Resources and staffing levels, staff motivation and intentions, and other factors all contribute to the reality of the 'choice' as offered.

Learning-disabled people are powerless in these settings, at the mercy of often broken or under-resourced systems – and holding families at arm's length enables the quiet warehousing of people deemed to be troublesome and challenging.

My blog posts, which had been fairly forthright about the awful support available when Connor was at home, became more measured when he was in the Unit because of this fear of being distanced from him. Weary Mother, a regular contributor to my blog, captured this fear from the perspective of a parent who had been fighting her son's corner for decades:

> *What kind of world permits weary elderly parents to live crippled with fear of the next crises, and every minute with the bigger fear of raising the issue with a nasty and failing public organisation?*
>
> *Old parents have lived long with pared down lives, and are now increasingly deep in anxiety and stress from filling many dangerous gaps in care. Very often a sole old parent broken down with additional fear to question anything for it will routinely produce a dangerous and childish petulance that rebounds on son/daughter.*

Before Connor went into the Unit my determination for him to do something with his life rather than sink into a nothingness of YouTube-watching with no fresh air, exercise or social stuff was mainly because I knew that with the right support he was capable of working. And because we all have to do things we don't necessarily want to do.

I'd been looking into the possibility of setting up a social enterprise scheme around a mobile shredding van. Connor was fascinated with recycling, and I thought that one of his more openly sociable school mates could do the picking-up of documents and chatting with punters, while Connor shredded them in the back of the van. There would be no risk of any documentation not shredded or content discussed; Connor would be utterly diligent, and it could generate some community interaction if the van had regular spots around the area.

All that was needed was the van, a shredding machine and a third team member to drive to the various pick-up points and oversee the work. Sadly, the relentless focus on indicative budgets by social care left no one to ask about how to go about setting up such a venture. I was in the process of talking with other parents via Twitter, and existing social enterprise organisers, when Connor went downhill.

I now wish I'd got a bank loan for the van and shredder and just gone ahead with the idea, finding out information as we went along. At that point I was swamped, with no information about how such a venture could be set up, an increasingly anxious Connor and the yawning black hole of a future he was facing.

Epilepsy reaches the Unit

On 20 May 2013, Day 63 of Connor's time at the Unit, I found him lying on his bed looking disorientated.

He had bitten his tongue and had clearly had a seizure. He must have told someone about his tongue because Dr Murphy, the consultant psychiatrist, prescribed Bonjela. Either she did not consider an epileptic seizure, or she discounted a seizure without recording it in the records, despite the fact that Connor had documented sensitivity to medication change (generating seizures) and she had recently changed his medication.

I alerted the staff on duty, phoned later that evening to make sure the night staff were aware I thought he had experienced a seizure, and emailed the Unit manager to let Dr Murphy and Dr Jayawant know. At Connor's inquest, the student nurse who answered the phone that night said I was crying. I don't remember, it was all so awful.

Staff seemed to respond swiftly, moving Connor to a downstairs bedroom next to the nurses' office the following day and increasing their observations. Charlotte Sweeney, the occupational therapist, phoned me to talk about ordering a seizure monitor. I felt some reassurance, though I remained sick at the thought of him enduring a seizure with no one to comfort him.

The weeks passed with little apparent activity or action on the part of social services or Southern Health. Connor was no longer sectioned by now but he was still agitated and there was no support organised for him to come home. There was also little attention paid to his status as an informal patient (a patient who has agreed to stay in hospital voluntarily, and so not detained under the Mental Health Act).

A 'best interest assessor' came to assess whether Connor was being deprived of his liberty after his section was lifted. He rang me in the evening to say Connor was restricted but not deprived of his liberty because he wasn't trying to abscond when out of the Unit, was offered regular options to leave the Unit on outings – which he regularly turned down – and hadn't said he wanted to leave, although he did tell the best interest assessor he didn't want to be there. His conclusion was that, apart from the locked door, there was nothing stopping Connor leaving. I didn't know what to say to this. It struck me as gibberish.

We took Connor out at weekends and, on 9 June 2013, we took him to London for the day with Tom. It was not a good day. We ended up driving round Camden looking for Dappy from N-Dubz, a hip hop group he loved, to try to calm Connor down.

On the motorway coming back, Connor began hitting himself in the face so hard, he ended up with a terrible nosebleed. The next day a 'Care Plan Approach' meeting was held – a meeting to discuss and assess Connor's health and social care needs involving him, his family and the professionals involved in his care. It was a deeply frustrating meeting which got us no further forward. From the minutes:

Mum said that she was confused that CS [Connor Sparrowhawk] was admitted to STATT [the Unit] for assessment and treatment, but where is the assessment and treatment? Dr Murphy explained that CS is not the usual type of patient we have on STATT. He is in a transition stage, and is slightly younger than our usual patients. Working with school is unusual too, and CS has been here longer than our usual patients would be.

A couple of weeks later on 25 June I wrote the following post:

We passed the 100 day mark this week. 100 days. 100 days of incarceration. …leaving sounds are being made. Most vocally by LB. The slow wheels of social care are groaning into a 'let's talk about potential provision at some vague meeting at some unspecified point in the near-ish future' position. I suspect (sadly) this may be quite something in social care activity terms in the case of young dudes like LB.

Incarceration came about because there was no care or support available. This [incarceration] has given us – er, I'm making some unsubstantiated assumptions here – a slightly better position in terms of access to support. I'm less than optimistic about what that support might look like, given anecdotal and other information, but the bar is set so low from where we are, support of any shape that actually supports, is progress.

Reading between the lines (because nothing is transparent here) unnamed people (in health/social care/education?) are aware that LB is ready and in need of support to enable him to be released from the (I'm assuming) costly provision he's been an inmate of for the last 100 or so days. Not that he's locked up or anything.

Now there's the rub. For the first time, we're insisting on effective and appropriate support. This position makes me feel slightly heady, slightly hysterical, hugely enraged but mainly sad.

But hey. What about LB? How's he doing?

Three things jump out this week.

1. He attended the emotions group, which was progress after the first meeting when he turned up, gave everyone the finger and left.

2. He's asked me repeatedly this week if he's mainstream now.

3. When I ring and they pass the phone to him, he has a nifty exchange with me – 'Yeah, right.' 'Yeah, cool, see you then.' 'Right, yes, cool, yeah.'

I'd take these three things as a sign that there is some shaking down in his mind of who he is, and what he wants.

C'mon social care (if you hold the power here). Let's act on that and create him a space in which to live productively. And, while I'm at it, can I chuck back into the mix the feelings of siblings who are offered no support, and, if under 16, not allowed to visit their brother or sister on site?

It shouldn't be like this.

On Monday 1 July,[5] unable to attend the weekly team meeting, I emailed the Unit's administrator:

Can I send my apologies today because I can't get out of work, but I just wanted to say that Connor seems to be quite apathetic and not very responsive in the last few days. I don't know if the staff think that?

Thanks,

Sara

---

5   A meeting was arranged with Southern Health, Oxfordshire County Council, education and the commissioners for 8 July to arrange support for Connor to come home.

The minutes of that meeting I missed suggest my concerns were raised and dismissed; the meeting notes we received after Connor's death stated: 'No one specifically noted this.' No. No one noticed anything like that. Nothing to see here. Moving on to the next patient...

We later found out it was recorded in Connor's electronic notes in a couple of places that he had been quiet, red eyed and subdued over that weekend (at school, Connor's teachers would often flag up points at which he seemed subdued or clammy as pointers that he may be about to have a seizure). The staff on duty were not typically staff attending the weekly team meeting and no one bothered to check the records in response to my email.

No one bothered.

The next day I took my parents to visit Connor. It was the last time we saw him alive. The next evening I was at a work seminar.

Rich visited Connor and they watched some tennis together. Andy Murray was playing Fernando Verdasco in the Wimbledon quarter final.

PART II

AFTERMATH

CHAPTER 4

The Fallout

The relatives room

The relatives room. John Radcliffe Hospital. 4 July 2013. A bare, nondescript space which must bear witness to devastation and incomprehension like few other spaces in the NHS. I can only detail the basic chronology of that morning.

I was taken to where Connor was so that the machine mechanically keeping him breathing could be turned off. Someone, possibly a paramedic, went with me and explained what I would see and what would happen. It was brutal.

Rich was contacted at the town hall by someone from the hospital who made it clear something serious had happened.

Mary, my friend who worked in A&E, was driven by a colleague to collect Rosie, who was at home from university.

Caroline, my colleague, waited for Rich to arrive, then went back to work, told colleagues what had happened and went home.

Rich rang my mum from the car park where there was a signal. She hung up on him.

Rich and Rosie drove to Tom's school. He was taken out of class to the headteacher's office and told what had happened. Will drove himself and Owen over from Henley, hungover from Owen's 18th birthday celebrations the night before.

The hospital staff were exceptional. Tissues, space and sugary tea on tap. I don't remember very much at all about being with Connor when the machine was turned off that morning. Rosie, Rich and I went to see him a bit later. He still had the resuscitation equipment in place. The handling of the 'organ donation' conversation, which happened so fucking swiftly, was exemplary.

'Yes. Yes, of course.'

Connor's heart valves were taken for children's heart surgery. I don't know why. I just like to think those kids, or that kid, whoever they are, have somehow captured some of his magic and eccentricity.

We went home.

Death decisions

Connor was dead. Dead. The ease, the physicality, the being. The being someone. Alive. A life. How could he be dead? He was in a fucking NHS hospital with almost one-to-one care… He was locked up and never came home.

What to do? What do you do? What the fuck do you do when your greatest fear is realised? Life outside Connor's death stopped. There was no 'stages of grief' bollocks or complicated grief crap. Just raw grief with fucking chips on top.

Family and friends started to turn up. Rosie's mates pitched up via the Co-op with bags of sliced bread and bacon and started cooking. They seemed to have a headstart on knowing what to do, in a space in which none of us knew what to do.

Days and nights became irrelevant as I'd fall asleep on the settee only to wake an hour or so later, and for the briefest of moments not remember that Connor was dead. I hated those moments. Taunting moments too fleeting to seize hold of for a break from the anguish and terror.

I'd lay awake at night tormented by what had happened and missing Connor with an indescribable intensity. I ached to see him, to touch him, to smell him. To hear his voice and answer his questions. Often I would get up, vomit words on my blog and press 'save' or 'publish'. This generated some piercingly painful posts, many of which are not public, but the writing of the horror, the grief, the despair allowed me to fall into bed and sleep for a while.

Some people got in touch to say that such frank and uncensored outpourings were helpful to them. I've no idea if I will revisit the unpublished posts. I suspect they will remain saved electronically – an alternative form of a traditional handwritten paper diary, stored in the equivalent of a dusty loft somewhere.

Rosie and I sat up into the early hours of the morning, writing lists, weeping, glugging beer and wine (me more than Rosie), sobbing and writing: funeral lists, things to do, people to contact, decisions to make. Horrible, huge, cavernous death decisions which are the worst decisions imaginable, pushing and poking us into spaces that scream, 'DANGER.' Spaces we'd dipped into, around other people's deaths, vicariously over the years. Fictional and real-life examples that would touch us, fleetingly, for moments or longer, while we were secure and cocky in the knowledge that unexpected, untimely, nasty, preventable death, and the darkness that comes with it, would never touch us.

Now decisions needed to be made in what still seemed like only minutes since Connor died. Rich, love him, dealt with the practicalities, though there were some unavoidable, unspeakable conversations to be had with the funeral directors.

'Would you prefer burial or cremation for Connor?'

'Eh?'

'Would you prefer burial or cremation?' I don't want either. *Please, stop this now.*

[Gagged silence]

'I'm sorry but you will have to make this decision soon...' No. *I can't think about this.*

'If you want a burial we will need to find an available space. The Oxford cemeteries are quite full.' He is 18. He was *getting ready to visit the Oxford Bus Company...* 'He. Can't. *Be. Incinerated.'*

'Leave it with us. We will see what spaces are available in the local cemeteries...'

We spent hours poring over and choosing family photos to make a short film for Connor's funeral, and re-watched a video interview I'd done with our research assistant the afternoon before Connor died. It was the first time I was interviewed about being Connor's mum and was simply to provide interview practice. Colleagues brought this film round to us as soon as they could; carrying the random preciousness of talk about Connor in the present tense on a memory stick.

A human rights intervention

An unexpected outcome of writing the blog was the support it opened up to us after Connor died. Human rights barrister Caoilfhionn Gallagher from Doughty Street Chambers – a law firm renowned for and committed to defending freedom and civil liberties – contacted me via Twitter a day or so after Connor died and said we should be prepared that Connor's death might not be effectively investigated, despite it happening within the NHS. She suggested we contact INQUEST, a small charity that provides free advice to people bereaved by a death in custody or detention. Within days we were talking to an INQUEST caseworker, Selen Cavcav, who reiterated Caoilfhionn's advice and said we would need legal representation to ensure that Connor had a fair inquest hearing.

In a short space of time, we'd instructed a leading human rights solicitor, Charlotte Haworth Hird from Bindmans LLP, to represent us and Caoilfhionn had offered pro bono support. Around the same time Paul Bowen QC, a barrister at Brick Chambers, also offered his support. We were in our brutalised and barely standing state, overwhelmed and grateful for these offers of help, without realising how crucial they would be.

Without Caoilfhionn's intervention we would have been reliant on a lacklustre leaflet from the Coroner's office and would have assumed that a rigorous process was in place to ensure effective scrutiny into and examination of what had happened, and why. Some Trusts, I'm sure, must investigate deaths effectively, but the evidence generated since Connor's death, and as an outcome of his death, suggests to me that, too often, they are not.

We came to learn much later how Southern Health used their experience of dealing with unexpected deaths and the coronial system to ensure measures were in place to reduce the whiff of accountability. We had no idea how uneven the 'playing field' was in a game we didn't yet understand we were playing.

Post-death work

I sat on the phone to Selen in the kitchen, my notebook slowly filling with largely illegible scrawl. After Selen, a phone conversation with our newly appointed solicitor Charlotte, who carefully outlined further things that needed attention: request Connor's medical records as soon as possible and make sure the pathologist conducted his post-mortem using the Royal College of Pathology guidelines for epilepsy.[1]

There is no post-death peace when an unexpected death happens in the 'care' of the NHS. There is no equivalent of a police liaison officer to provide support, advice and generally mop up some of the pieces. We were lucky to have advice from Charlotte, Selen and others. Most families will not

---

1   There are a set of processes that should be followed for an epilepsy-related death too grisly to recount here but involving the brain and brain tissue. The Royal College of Pathologists also offers a set of guidelines for alternative investigation in exceptional circumstances.

have someone to flag how systems and processes may not be followed, or that they might not work.

The cost of legal representation at Connor's inquest was going to be somewhere around a staggering £20,000. NHS trusts could spend any amount of public money on their legal representation but families have to pay their own costs. I kept scrawling. A sort of mechanical moving of pen to paper. Making marks. Writing to distract myself from being swallowed up by the horror of knowing that Connor was lying dead in a funeral home across the road to us. And to distance myself from the various details we were learning about what happens when a child or relative dies an unexpected death in the care of the NHS.

It was Tom's 14th birthday a week after Connor's death and we dragged ourselves in to town to get him a present. Passing the funeral home on the way back I realised that Connor must have gone to hospital that morning without any clothes on after being found in the bath. Christ. Fuck. Jesus fucking H Christ. My beautiful boy was lying there dead and naked. A silent scream ricocheted around my frazzled and exhausted brain.

We later discovered that the pathologist hadn't followed the guidelines relating to possible epilepsy-related death, and as a result Charlotte was concerned that the resulting conclusion of 'unascertained death' was a serious problem. We needed to request a second post-mortem or, at the very least, to request a redoing of some of the original post-mortem. The former would involve delaying Connor's funeral.

No 'First Fit' clinic in life or death

The next day, at Charlotte's suggestion, I rang the Coroner's officer. It was a scrambled and touching on hysterical interaction, and I eventually spoke to the pathologist who conducted Connor's post-mortem. I still remember the call, standing outside our back door in a baking hot garden, shadowed memories of Connor basking in the sunshine, absorbed in a map of London on the grass. The house full of people, food and flowers.

The pathologist 'believed' he had followed Royal College guidelines. The Coroner's office said guidelines were 'guidelines' and that brain tissue in epilepsy cases wasn't routinely sampled because it rarely revealed anything. I listened while scrutinising the pebble dash on the wall. It was done by a mate of a mate as part of the extension years earlier, and our neighbour said he didn't think it was done well enough to stand the test of much time.

I don't know if Connor's medical notes or route of entry into the mortuary were flagged with 'Seriously, don't bother, he doesn't count' in some sort of shorthand, but it struck me that there was little consideration of his epilepsy during his post-mortem, just as there had been little or none during his time at the Unit.

It would have been so 'easy' to say we didn't want any more intrusion. Without Charlotte Haworth Hird's meticulous attention, we would never have known that the post-mortem wasn't conducted properly. At that point, a 'head in the sand' approach was so appealing given the horror of even beginning to think about subjecting Connor to further brutality.

A line from one of Charlotte's emails said:

'I am sorry to be so blunt but I want to be sure that you can make an informed decision.'

Informed decision making. A concept that rarely, if ever, entered the world of health and social care in relation to learning disability from our experience. Reading or hearing information or decisions which made sense, as we were to do every now again across the next few years, came as a wrench, shaking us from the shite we'd been battered into accepting, over years of crap support.

After considerable agitation and discussion, we agreed on the least intrusive of Charlotte's suggestions to rescue the robustness of the post-mortem examination. Connor would be taken back to the John Radcliffe for one further test, then returned to the funeral home across the road.

Rich and I walked to and from the funeral home over the next week or so. Past the park, shops and shoppers; families, kids and dogs; people busying about, shopping in Iceland; catching the bus into town. All doing stuff. All going somewhere. I can't remember what we talked about. Maybe we didn't talk.

Those days, pre-funeral, were so strange. The funeral home staff were sensitive, kind and prepared to open at the weekend so we could keep visiting. Again, an experience that defies words but it was something we felt compelled to do. At the funeral home, his body was presented in different ways. The first, and most harrowing, was before his coffin was made and he was laid out on a bed, fully dressed. The funeral home had warned us that his coffin wasn't ready but I didn't realise what this meant in terms of visiting him. When the coffin was finished (it was truly beautiful), we visited when the coffin was closed and open, with a lace covering over the top.

I think it depends on who is working on how the body is displayed. I'm not a lace fan but think the latter was probably the 'best' way to visit Connor. It's remarkable how quickly someone looks different once they are dead. Skin, hair and body change within hours, and by the funeral home stage, it is almost mannequin like.

The first time we went, I went prepared to hang out all afternoon with Connor. I didn't know what else to do really. As it was, it wasn't really him and, while we visited daily, we didn't stay long. It was a bit like how I feel now with the cemetery. I had visions of picnics by Connor's woodland graveside like the Fowler family on *EastEnders*, long afternoons with a flask of tea and a book, keeping vigil like Chunky Stan did, waiting for Connor's bus each morning. But there is nothing to wait for.

I spent hours in the garden that summer staring at the sky, late into the evening, searching for something, some sort of understanding or way of making sense of what had happened, weeping or walking in the park with the dogs.

Friends and family came round, bringing food and booze and doing their best to do their best, without any guidelines. The postman knocked daily with bundles of cards parcelled with four-way elastic bands. Comforting bands that didn't allow slippage.

There were deliveries of flowers two or three times a day for days on end. Rich went to the local hardware shop to buy more vases.

Connor's do

Connor's funeral, his 'do', was, in retrospect, spectacular. 'Life-raft' mates Becca, Fran and the rest of the gang whose kids had been at Connor's school took on the responsibility for organising it. They managed to negotiate the trickiest of tricky territory with sensitivity, skill and persistence. They would appear in our kitchen with a clipboard, ask key questions, and then disappear, scouring the county for a venue that was available, suitable and not prohibitively pricey. Not an easy task with such short notice. On the Monday afternoon, with just over a week to go before the planned service, they pitched up, nervously.

> *'We've found a possibility but thought it was best to take you to see it... Can you pop out now to have a quick look? It's not far...'*

> *'It's a big enough space. The manager is incredibly helpful. Her son died a few years ago and she's furious about what's happened. It's available as long as we're out before an evening booking...'*

> *'On first sight, it may look a bit shabby...'*

> *'Yes, the entrance is a bit dark and dated but there's potential...'*

I got in the car, vaguely surprised to see a world beyond the park and funeral home, while they continued to sell this mysterious venue and, simultaneously, prime me for disappointment. We drove towards the ring road and a random thought popped into my mind.

'You don't mean the Cowley Works place?'

'Er, yeah. It's a bit dated but…'

'Aww. That's a bloody brilliant idea. We went to a kids' footy award evening there years ago; Rosie gave out the prizes when Rich was away. It's perfect. Connor would love it…'

The relief was palpable. An enormous ballroom-type space and cheap bar, a throwback to the 1970s, with playing fields as far as you could see. A perfect venue for something that should never have to happen. Funeral organisation continued and the clipboard was on fire as Becca and gang managed to hire a vintage Routemaster double-decker bus from BBC Radio 2 DJ Ken Bruce's bus company to take people to and from the cemetery instead of funeral cars. Catering, sound and music all sorted.

The day of the funeral arrived: dreaded, dark and suffocating. I walked around the park early morning. Being outside and moving helped to slightly ease the terror and distress. I thought about carrying Connor's blood sample[2] from our GP surgery next to the park to the John Radcliffe Hospital 16 years earlier.

I remember pushing Connor in his pushchair, with the sample swinging on the handle almost in tune to one of the Barney songs. Tromping across the park. Through the Headington alleyways into the John Radcliffe grounds. An open-and-anything-could-happen journey. I mean anything could have unfolded at that point. A young tot, diagnoses a go-go brewing, but still a little person. An individual. With rights and expectations.

---

2   This revealed Connor had a mosaic form of a chromosome disorder called Klinefelter syndrome.

It was already baking hot. Later that morning I took a photo of Rosie, Will, Owen and Tom in the kitchen dressed in smart, bright colours. All looking completely and utterly sideswept while managing to just about smile.

All I could see in taking that photo was a flickering slide show of the thousands of photos I'd taken of the five of them: hugging each other on a long walk in Pembrokeshire; a brief walk on the beach during a relentlessly rainy holiday in Devon when we ended up watching back-to-back Olympics; numerous Christmas mornings, spats and fun times; banter and birthdays; the steamy bus in London heading for the Tower; visiting the Imperial War Museum where Connor wouldn't leave the Routemaster bus in the foyer.

Now they were about to walk behind their brother's coffin to his graveside and somehow pick up their lives afterwards.

Rich and I are beyond proud of how they seem to have dealt with what happened with such strength, decency and kindness, supported by exceptional friends.

The bus began at the Cowley Works and pulled up outside our house early afternoon. It seemed sort of unexpected, because there is no 'expected' for the funeral of an 18-year-old boy. Rich had gone to Peacocks up the road to buy Tom a shirt. I was in the garden. Someone shouted that the bus had arrived.

It was time.

Few things can be as sad as burying your child.

The funeral director had organised a beautiful, shiny Routemaster coffin for Connor. He was to be driven home, as he had wanted to be for those 107 days spent at the Unit, to begin his journey to the cemetery. Friends and family waited for the hearse. A crowd mingled in the street. Talking quietly, standing, crying. Nipping in to use the toilet.

The hearse arrived with the brilliant red coffin framed like a jewel, or a die-cast model in a glass case in the model shop. We boarded the bus. A woman who lives down the road walked past. She clearly didn't know. She looked up and caught my eye as we sat in our seats upstairs at the front of the bus. Her face was a picture of utter shock and sadness.

The funeral director slowly walked in front of the hearse, stepping out into the traffic on the London Road. He parted the sea of buses and cars, usually edgy with impatience, with an authoritative stillness and slowly walked across the carriageway into the right-hand lane. All those days and evenings Connor had spent watching this constant traffic out of his bedroom window. Here he was, stopping it.

Bus drivers, passengers and drivers waited silently for the funeral director on foot, the hearse with the Routemaster coffin, the vintage double-decker bus and procession of cars behind to pass.

Ten minutes or so later we pulled up outside the cemetery where there seemed to be crowds of people. The tears that just wouldn't stop meant I couldn't see much other than splashes of colour. People were dressed for a summer party. A friend was waiting at the gate and hugged me before the humanist minister stepped forward to give us an intense 'You can do this. Do not pass out' stare. We slowly walked behind the hearse, along the winding drive to the woodland section in the far-right-hand corner of the cemetery.

Connor's support teacher Big Sue and another teaching assistant, Tina, who had stood next to Connor onstage singing *What a Wonderful World* all those years before, had asked to be pallbearers. We didn't know that they and the funeral home staff had arranged to dress in red and blue like bus drivers. They carefully carried Connor to his graveside under the trees where the short ceremony was conducted.

Rich said a few words and then a friend sat under a tree and played *Here Comes the Sun* on their guitar. I get goosebumps whenever I hear this song now, typically played by buskers in Oxford city centre. The kids had collected together Connor's collection of bus tickets from his room and people scattered bus tickets, or petals from Catherine's garden, into his grave.

Crowds of people came. Family, friends, the kids' friends, neighbours, Connor's classmates, teachers, people from various local charities and organisations, friends and colleagues from both universities, and even someone from Twitter who I had never met before in person. On the bus journey back to the Cowley Works, a playlist included songs like *Summer Holiday*, *Big Yellow Taxi* and *Summer Breeze*. No detail was too small for this do.

On that journey along the ring road I experienced an odd feeling of relief, or maybe release, and the tears stopped for a while.

Back at the Cowley Works, Becca and team had upped food production as we called 'team sarnie' from the cemetery to say there was a shedload of people. We hung out, drank and shared stories of Connor while the bus driver stayed to let kids play on the bus in the car park and footy was played in the playing fields.

We asked people to write down any memories or thoughts they had about Connor on cards. Here are a few:

First, the swearing…

On Rosie's 14th birthday: Connor swearing under his breath.

Connor's dad: 'Connor, stop swearing!'

A few seconds of silence pass.

Connor continuing under his breath: 'Wanker.'

On another occasion:

We had a new dinner system at school. Wristbands for meat or veg (no menus). I said to Connor, 'Do you want the meat or veg option for lunch?' 'What will I eat?' asked Connor. 'I don't know. There is no menu, just a band.' 'This is bollocks, isn't it?' I couldn't agree more.

He would often swear under his breath or gesticulate in ways that led you to wonder whether or not you had imagined it, it could be so subtle. There was a period one summer when he took to standing in the front garden, talking to himself and flicking the Vs at any passing car. Luckily it was short lived.

Then, Connor's imagination…

My beautiful, beautiful Connor. You came into school and said, 'L, I got arrested last night!' I said, 'Oh no, Connor, what on earth have you done?' 'I got caught behind the back of the youth club smoking marijuana.' 'Oh dear, Connor.' I love you. x

Connor. What a fantastic dude. Not many are able to bring light and laughter to every situation, but Connor succeeded on a daily basis.

Connor could also spin a convincing yarn, or ten. At one point, he was telling school that we kept him in the cupboard under the stairs, feeding him bread and water. A more believable story is that he had Chinese takeaway containers under his bed. Like the voices he drew on in his early morning chatter, he captured different strands of actual events and wove these into his imagination, producing colourful accounts of what had, or hadn't, happened to him.

His love, honesty and openness:

Connor said the nicest thing any child has ever said to me because it was so spontaneous. The conversation went like this: 'Connor, will you pick up those beanbags.' Connor moaned and refused. I was irritable and hot (not that I usually was). 'Connor, I am the teacher in charge whether you like it or not.' A long pause. 'I like it.'

So privileged to have known such a lovely young man. I knew Connor when he would always go and do the litter picking at school. He was so responsible and would come back at the specified time agreed. He taught me how responsible these secondary school children could be, with gentle nurturing and direction from the staff. He would also always be checking at the classroom door when we were tube-feeding pupils. He had his beady eye on us. Fond memories. Rest easy Connor, you were great.

And the fun:

'Who do you like best Connor, Stan or Bess?' 'Stan.' 'Stan or Richard?' 'Stan.' 'Stan or John?' 'John.' At least that's how John remembers it. Connor will always be at the top of our list. I feel so lucky to have known him. xx

Fond memories of Connor. We hope the buses where you are, are running on time. xxx

I was on the Oxford Tube coach, on my way to a meeting in London earlier, thinking about that time you made an announcement about suicide bombers. We were on a day out in London with Rosie and Tom, a few weeks after the July bombings.

You said in such an unexpectedly deep voice:

'Can any suicide bombers please make themselves known to the driver!'

There was a stunned silence.

Then Tom's tooth fell out and he asked me for a tissue.

'A tissue? Who do you think I am? Supermum?'

We hadn't reached the Thornhill Park and Ride.

CHAPTER 5

Death of a Service User

At this stage, we had no idea what we didn't know but should have known. We had no idea that Connor's death would generate a groundbreaking social movement and lead to the uncovering of systematic failure to investigate the deaths of certain patients in the UK. We had no idea of the fight that lay ahead, or the amount of blame that would be chucked my way.

Unknown to us, in the midst of this early grief and horror, 'reputation repair work' had kicked into action big time at both Oxfordshire County Council (who paid for the service at the Unit) and Southern Health NHS Foundation Trust (who provided it). They were speedily careering along on separate and discordant tracks trying to wriggle out of any responsibility for what had happened.[1] The day after

1   We were to piece this together retrospectively after making Subject Access Requests (SAR) to each of the relevant organisations. You can request information in which you are mentioned under section 7 of the Data Protection Act 1998, specifying the search terms and the period of time you would like covered. This revealed email exchanges among senior County Council officials about potential press interest. See https://ico. org.uk/for-organisations/guide-to-data-protection/principle-6-rights/ subject-access-request

Connor's death, Southern Health circulated a document among several recipients, redacted when we received it, entitled *Potential Media Interest – Background Briefing on Mother's Blog.*[2] After a chilling intro about a 'Learning Disabilities SU' (service user), the briefing continues:

> *We were made aware that a blog, containing details of our staff on the unit by [redacted] in March. It was agreed that [redacted] would monitor the blog and raise any potential issues as previously the entries had mentioned staff by name and had been potentially defamatory towards staff.*

There was no reflection on the substance of the blog which highlighted issues relating to Connor's life and care. The focus was solely on the potential impact on their reputation. Southern Health was originally a Hampshire-based Trust, which merged with Oxfordshire Learning Disabilities Trust in 2012. You would think that their antenna would be on heightened alert for any potential problems in their new structure.

The blog briefing continued with the focus on me:

> *Blog entries concerning Connor's stay at an inpatient unit started on day one of his admission on 20 March 2013 and have been regularly updated since.*
>
> *Blog entries are generally around her academic and professional entries in learning disabilities and mental health, as well as a personal interest in photography. Posts relating to Connor vary from an account of a visit or day in very general*

---

2   We received this document in October 2014 via a BBC journalist. Southern Health did not disclose it to us despite the SAR we submitted to the Trust.

terms, to specific detailed complaints about the service he has received either generally or from specific members of staff.

Whereas blog posts relating to the STATT [Unit] service Connor in were number [sic] on the days he has been there, she often refers to health and social care services generally about the support she has sought for Connor throughout his life. Some key themes she refers to are of patient choice, and the controversial view that the service shouldn't always give him the choice not to go out or attend activities, and that in some cases he should be made to do things. In earlier posts, there is also the alarm that Connor has the right to say no, or yes, to things he does or doesn't want.

I'll leave the reader to ponder over the wording of this document: the 'othering' of Connor's family and the implicit blame that I read it to be coated in. The post I wrote after Connor's seizure in May was highlighted as potentially problematic:

Depending on the reason of death and the events leading up to the incident, there may be some concerns raised by the mother on Day 63 (21 May 2013) which she may revisit.

This post was reproduced in full; the saddest 150-odd words that were to become a key part of the evidence during Connor's inquest.

He was in bed, dozing. With a bitten swollen tongue. Signs of a seizure. Or size of an elephant it might well have been.

The bitten tongue had been noted and Bonjela on order. The seizure dimension overlooked. LB's seizures have always worried the pants off me. Not least because it took about four *'in your face' tonic-clonic epics before the docs would even entertain the idea that he might have epilepsy. We were tripping over that old 'he's got to learn to manage his stress/star charts anyone?' chestnut (aka. the learning disability trump card) for months.*

The thought of him having a seizure, in a locked unit, unnoticed, has generated a new level of distress I can't describe. I don't care how old he is, and I certainly ain't treating him like a child, but I want to comfort him, and keep a watchful eye for any further seizures. And I can't.

No one involved in the production of this briefing, or who received a copy of it, appears to have stepped up to challenge it in any way. Something along the lines of:

'Er, I really don't think this is appropriate. A young man died in our care. I think we should be looking into exactly what has happened, not focusing on a blog his mother wrote.'

No one.

Mother-blame

I'd like to take a brief pause here to reflect on a core strand of this story, mother-blame.

Mother-blame is well documented in research and writings; in particular, the notorious work by Bruno Bettelheim, a psychiatrist writing several decades ago. He suggested that autism was caused by cold, unfeeling and rejecting 'refrigerator' mothers, a theory that has been resoundingly discredited but which seems to have the virulence of ground elder weed. Mothers (typically) are expected to care for our children without making a fuss about non-existent or crap services and support. If we dare speak up, on behalf of our children, we're labelled as 'hostile' or 'toxic'.

Paula Caplan, a clinical and research psychologist, who wrote *Don't Blame Mother*[3] in 1989, did some earlier research and found that mothers were blamed for virtually every kind of psychological or emotional problem that brought patients to see therapists. She revisited her work in 2013[4] and found that most of the basic principles that concerned her in the book still applied. More recently, an interdisciplinary edited collection[5] was published again highlighting how the mother blame game continues to thrive.

There are examples of mother-blame in the records disclosed to us after Connor's death as well as the documents produced and circulated since. Within the briefing on my blog produced in July 2013, the use of words such as 'The mother', 'her' or 'she', my 'controversial' views around choice, my 'alarm' about Connor's autonomy, and the 'potentially defamatory' statements I made suggest blame. It's a subject I'll return to later in the story.

CQC report and inquiries

For some reason, you have to pick up the belongings of someone who has died in an inpatient, or independent living,

3   Caplan, P. (1989) *Don't Blame Mother: Mending the Mother–Daughter Relationship.* HarperCollins.

4   Caplan, P. (2013) 'Don't Blame Mother: Then and Now.' In M.H. Hobbs and C. Rice (eds) *Gender and Women's Studies in Canada: Critical Terrain.* Women's Press, pp.99–106.

5   Reimer, S. and Sahagian, S. (2015) *The Mother-Blame Game.* Demeter Press.

setting pretty much straight away. My mum, who took over communication with Southern Health immediately after Connor's death, went to the Unit with my sisters to collect his stuff. They came back, looking ashen, and put the boxes down in the hall.

They said the Unit was crawling with 'suits' that morning. We knew the police were looking into what happened but I assume these 'suits' included commissioners and senior Southern Health staff. Oxfordshire County Council and the Oxfordshire Clinical Commissioning Group jointly paid for patients to receive the health care provided by Southern Health.

We later heard from NHS England that patients were supported by the Unit staff. I dread to think what the patients saw or heard that morning and how Connor's death affected them.

Basic humanity, decency and sense were bafflingly absent in the responses to the family from health and social care professionals, who would themselves have been daughters, sons, mothers, fathers, brothers or sisters.

Six weeks after Connor's death the independent care regulator the Care Quality Commission (CQC) inspected the Unit and failed it on all ten domains inspected.[6] The inspection report, eventually published in November 2013, was a chilling read.

We now knew we had left Connor in a shitty unit, which turned out to be even shittier than we imagined. The report read like an inspection of a Victorian asylum; from no

6   The CQC is the independent regulator of health and social care provision in England; their inspectors go to different hospitals and care homes for two or three days at a time to examine the quality and safety of the provision.

engagement with patients to medicines out of date and not stored properly, to faeces on furniture:

> *Over the course of two days, we saw few social or therapeutic nursing interactions with people who stayed there. There appeared to be an impoverished environment with little therapeutic intervention or meaningful activities to do.*

> *The pharmacist found that medicines were not always safely administered. Expiry date checking was not carried out adequately, the emergency oxygen was significantly out of date, and appropriate arrangements were not in place for the storage of medicines. We inspected the emergency equipment, and found some of it was not working.*

> *The defibrillator on John Sharich House[7] had no battery inside it. This meant that, in the event of a cardiac arrest, this defibrillator would not be able to be used for emergency treatment. We checked the oxygen cylinder in the clinical room. It had expired in June 2012. This meant that, in the event of an emergency requiring the administration of oxygen, no oxygen would be immediately available.[8]*

Phil Gayle, breakfast presenter at BBC Radio Oxford, first covered the story with his team at this point. I can still hear the incredulity in his voice as he questioned the Trust and County Council bods live on his show:

> *'There were faeces in a drawer…in 21st-century Britain…'*

---

7   A second unit on the same site as the STATT Unit Connor was in.

8   www.cqc.org.uk/sites/default/files/old_reports/RW11V_Slade_House_INS1-927131809_Scheduled_21-11-2013.pdf

The Trust was to argue retrospectively that the police hampered their efforts to see what was happening in the Unit, and that they mistakenly accepted the reassurances given by the Unit team. A new level of the 'dog ate my homework' type excuse.

Introducing 'natural causes'

After Connor's death, the familiar became unfamiliar and we inhabited a space layered with grief, darkness and disbelief. Not disbelief that Connor was dead – it was more than clear he was – but disbelief that he could have been allowed to die. After years of additional vigilance, of always making sure he was OK, of always looking out for him, I was utterly bereft and raging that one of my cubs had been killed so cruelly and so unnecessarily. Rich and I repeatedly came back to the same point: if nothing else, we thought he was in a safe space with trained NHS health professionals looking after him.

We began to look more closely at the Trust, which we had not heard of before the day that Connor was admitted to the Unit. In online board papers dated 23 July 2013, just over two weeks after Connor's death, I came across this reference to him:

> *A Serious Incident Requiring Investigation (SIRI) occurred in one of the Trust's learning disability in-patient facilities, leading to the unexpected death of a service user. The post-mortem indicates the user died of natural causes and early investigations indicate all appropriate systems and processes were in place and being followed leading up to the incident; however a full investigation is underway, in line with the Trust's agreed policy. Support has been offered to the family and*

to staff at the Unit. The Trust has informed commissioners, CQC and Monitor.[9]

The user...? Natural causes? At this stage, Connor's post-mortem was still under way. This reference to 'natural causes' buried on page 83 of over 200 pages of board minutes was bewildering and chilling.

'What do they mean by natural causes?'

'I don't know. The post-mortem isn't finished.'

'Why would they write that in their board papers?'

'I don't know.'

'It doesn't make any sense. We don't know how he died yet...'

There was never a satisfactory explanation from the Trust as to why this statement was published in the board papers. Simon Waugh, then Board Chair, wrote to me in 2014 saying that the Trust had not been able to trace where the use of this statement originated as it did not form part of any email correspondence. He went on to write:

'Whilst I am aware of how much distress this has caused you, I am entirely confident that there was no intention to distort the facts of the case.'

---

9   www.southernhealth.nhs.uk/about/who/board/board-meetings/
     2013-14-board-papers/?assetdete37a05e7-b96b-44ae-873c-df980edd
     772a=73017

He elaborated in his letter that it was probably an attempt by a non-clinical staff member to 'communicate there was no immediate evidence of foul play or suicide'.

Even if we take this response at face value, we were starting to uncover what we felt to be a persistent theme: the fobbing off of responsibility or blaming of others for failures when responsibility should lay with the Trust's executive board. Published Trust papers should have been approved by the board. It's as simple as that. And the idea that a fit and healthy young man could, while getting ready to go to visit the Oxford Bus Company, die in a hospital bath and have his death discounted so glibly was outlandish.

While we were only starting to discover how learning-disabled people are treated in NHS care, our story was unfolding against a backdrop of several important developments.

Death by Indifference

Connor's death occurred only a month or so after publication of *The confidential inquiry into premature deaths of people with learning disabilities (CIPOLD)* report in March 2013.

This Inquiry had been commissioned following a Mencap campaign in 2007, Death by Indifference. Mencap launched the campaign to highlight the stories of six people who they believed had died unnecessarily, and whose deaths evidenced institutional discrimination within the NHS: that learning-disabled people get worse healthcare than non-disabled people. Its aim was to educate healthcare professionals of the potentially fatal consequences of failing to understand the needs of learning-disabled people.

It also came two years after the BBC documentary *Panorama* broadcast about Winterbourne View in 2011, which exposed the physical and psychological abuse of learning-disabled patients at the privately run assessment and treatment unit in Gloucestershire.

A week after Connor's death, the government announced it would not set up the mortality review board as recommended by CIPOLD to investigate the estimated 1200 premature deaths each year of learning-disabled people in England, because of cost implications.

The combination of the circumstances of Connor's death, the subsequent 'natural causes' statement in the board meeting minutes, the CIPOLD findings and the refusal of the government to take them seriously made it clear to us that people were dying prematurely with little scrutiny. At the same time, there is some irony that, despite the immediate concerns about and focus on reputation demonstrated by both the County Council and Trust, there was no immediate media interest in Connor's death.

He was a 'lad with learning disabilities' living in what people thought of for a long time as a 'care home' – a carelessness that illustrates how the personhood of learning-disabled people is dismissed. The death of an 18-year-old boy in an NHS specialist unit was lost in the disregard and indifference people labelled with learning disabilities experience.

It took nine months before what happened to Connor made national news.

Criticisms of Southern Health and its responses

After the CQC inspection of the Unit, further evidence was to emerge demonstrating that the NHS 'brand' does not guarantee good or safe care, which further underlined just how poor the level of 'acceptable' could be to those who commission these services.

This included more CQC inspections of Southern Health provision, an Oxfordshire County Council Quality Review conducted in November 2012 revealed by a Freedom of Information request, and leaked internal documents sent to us anonymously.

There was clear evidence of issues in the Oxfordshire provision before the Southern Health merger. A leaked internal County Council document from August 2012 one of the documents, sent to us anonymously, raised issues around the cleanliness and general repair of the Unit, the lack of clarity around care plans and the limited evidence of assessment and treatment.

In April 2016, we received a copy of an anonymous letter originally sent to the chief executive officer (CEO) of Southern Health, Katrina Percy, in 2011, which raised health and safety concerns. An independent health and safety consultant, Mike Holder, was appointed by Southern Health in 2011 to troubleshoot the safety issues raised in this letter. He handed in his notice two months later, in early 2012, when it became clear that the executive board was not prepared to act on, or even listen to, his concerns.

Mike Holder left detailed documentation about the risks he'd identified, in particular ligature (suicide by hanging) risks, across the Southern Health mental health units. In his resignation letter, he stated:

At present it is my professional opinion that Health and Safety is considered an adjunct to the Trust's core business rather than an integral element of it. This assumption is based on my experience with the Trust to date, the lack of resourcing applied to the management of health and safety and information governance with regards to the maintenance of statutory records.

An exchange about this documentation[10] between Mike Holder and the interim Director of Nursing in February 2012 demonstrates the lacklustre engagement of the executive board with the issue of safety and risk in their mental health provision. The interim Director countered his concerns about ligature risk with the statement:

The challenge is at what point do the Trust board say, this is the point at which we will have to tolerate a certain degree of risk?

Decades earlier, anthropologist Clifford Geertz[11] ruminated on the argument that, because complete objectivity is impossible in research, we might as well let our sentiments run loose. Geertz paraphrased the economist Robert Solow, who suggested this was akin to saying that, because a completely germ-free surgical theatre cannot be created, surgeons may as well operate in the sewer.

In my view, the interim Director's response was verging on this position.

---

10   Revealed through a Freedom of Information request around this letter.

11   Geertz, C. (1994) 'Thick Description: Toward an Interpretive Theory of Culture.' In M. McIntyre (ed.) *Readings in the Philosophy of Social Science* Cambridge, MA: MIT Press, pp.213–231.

Mike Holder responded, stating that the Trust *'had an absolute duty to ensure the safety of its patients, particularly those who are vulnerable'*. His resignation clearly signalled to us that he felt the Trust executive was not taking these risks seriously enough.

Dirty lenses and human rights

I've long raged against the lack of recognition of the value and sometimes brilliance that Connor and so many others bring to society. The 'learning disability goggles' often worn by health and social care services erase anything other than the learning disability label.

The criteria by which we conventionally measure success, including exam results, GCSEs, degrees, promotion and dosh, are not anything that would remotely capture Connor's strengths, abilities and talents. This is a reflection of the narrowness of the criteria rather than a measure of what Connor could or couldn't do.

He had a remarkable memory for people, places, buses, lorries, films and history and was generous, honest and loyal. The lack of markers to acknowledge and recognise these strengths led to him and his classmates being chucked into a deficit bin on reaching adulthood. Outside family, school and a few other pockets of brilliance, Connor followed the 'burden' trajectory as laid out by the paediatrician all those years before. It was hard not to.

This was in contrast to the rich and textured ways in which he contributed to everyday life and kept us thinking critically.

There was the time I left him in the car outside Somerfield one evening after school. I was, again, rushing in for something like milk. I grabbed the milk, paid and ran back to the car waving enthusiastically at Connor. He was looking at me but didn't wave. I waved more vigorously. He continued to look straight at me without moving. Part of me was thinking, *'Wave back Connor, c'mon matey. I look like a complete muppet...'*

He sat contentedly, probably listening to Steve Wright's afternoon show, and simply didn't lift his arm up to move it from side to side. I thought later that, of course, he didn't wave back – I'd told him I was just going to get milk and that I'd be straight back. My wave was a layer of unnecessary. For him to add to this would create more unnecessary layers. I remember chuckling at how he made me reflect on the banality of the act of waving and its overuse.

He had a range of interests, and a curiosity and fascination that was infectious. He loved school trips to the Horse of the Year Show, despite having no interest in horses, and would carry the glossy programme round with him for months. He was a strong defender of human rights, fairness and equality and despised the Conservatives with a passion.

There were spats still, as with any kids. Most notably with Connor they came when he was asked to do something that took him away from his current activity. He'd rant and rage and call on his legal team to issue injunctions. This was often around being told to empty the dishwasher, which was one of the jobs the kids did. He'd crash the plates and shout about the ways in which his human rights were being breached, even calling it slavery at times.

Our plates remain chipped. And Connor would have expected a strong, human-rights-based campaign around what happened to him.

PART III

SEEKING JUSTICE FOR LB

CHAPTER 6

The Seeds of Justice for LB

Getting accountability or justice for Connor's death was to be a gargantuan task as, just as we had been warned, Southern Health NHS Foundation Trust con-tinued the fight to protect its reputation. Nearly four months after Connor died, the Trust commissioned an independent investigation into what happened.

I've lost track of the myriad and circular conversations that Rich, I and others had at the time about the investigation, but they would go something like this:

'*Apparently the Trust will lead the investigation. It will take about four weeks and it looks like it will be led by the same person who did the quality review of the Unit back in November 2012.*'

'*An employee of the Trust? How the hell does that work?*'

'*No idea. Talk about marking your own homework. I suspect he goes in, pokes about a bit with his eyes closed, writes words on a page and circulates it to the Trust, local authority and commissioners. Nothing to see here.*'

'*But Connor died. There should be an independent investigation.*'

'*Yep.*'

As it was, the varying gradients of 'independence' proposed for the Trust-led investigation didn't materialise and they eventually appointed an independent consultancy called Verita in October 2013.

By this stage, I can only assume the County Council and commissioners were beginning to realise the ineptness, at best, of the glittering Trust they had only a year or so earlier thought would solve the problems of the failing Oxfordshire provision. Our concerns before the publication of the report were stacking up, partly as a result of our experiences and partly through the careful scrutiny of documentation from meetings generated by the Trust, with other reports and commentary coming from a growing number of people on social media.

This group, which became known as 'Team LB', included:

- Dr George Julian @georgejulian, a freelance knowledge transfer consultant, who became a central campaigner and worked tirelessly in pursuit of justice, bringing a remarkable and unusual expertise around social media use, engagement and analysis.

- Members of Oxfordshire self-advocacy group My Life My Choice[1] @mylifemychoice1, who wrote to our MP, the Trust and NHS England, met with Southern Health executive members and generally stood alongside us.

- Liz Piercy @Jesslinworld, an ex-NHS employee with a keen eye for detail and a heart for injustice, who curated all mention of Connor in the media. Liz examined the various numerous documents secured through Freedom of Information requests, logging key issues meticulously.

- Professor Chris Hatton @chrishattoncedr, an academic at Lancaster University, who has worked in the area of learning disability and public health for over 20 years. He conducted forensic examinations of Southern Health board minutes and published lay summaries of relevant data on a bespoke blog, 'Data for LB' (http://dataforlb.blogspot.co.uk).

- Agent T @TRogers1961, my older sister Tracey, who wrote letters to each board member asking searching questions and braved an early public board meeting to request that Southern Health amend the

---

1   This is a charity run by learning-disabled people.

'natural causes' comment in their board minutes (they never did).

- John Lish @losttransport, a Trustee of Waymarks, a charity that helps learning-disabled or autistic people with 'complex histories' change their lives. John offered measured and insightful advice and viewpoints.

- Mark Neary @markneary1, whose son Steven had been illegally detained in an assessment and treatment unit for a year and who wrote a frank blog about his experiences as Steven's father.

- Jenny Walker @jennywalkabout, mother of an adult son with learning disabilities, who kept us stocked with treats and encouragement.

Many more people offered support through my blog and via Facebook, and some time in February 2014 these streams coalesced into a '#JusticeforLB' campaign. George Julian stepped up to manage a #JusticeforLB blog, hashtag and Twitter feed, while other supporters pitched in with whatever they felt able to offer.

#JusticeforLB was born. At the start of the campaign there was a diverse range of people following what was happening on social media: social workers, students, academics from a range of disciplines, self-advocacy and advocacy groups, journalists, documentary film makers, charities, health professionals, parents and carers, and data protection and human rights specialists. This diversity was to be a strength in what unfolded.

Southern Health finally agreed for the Verita report *Independent investigation into the death of CS* to be published on 24 February 2014 after some meithering around the suggestion that a 'summary' of the report should be published instead of the actual report. The power imbalance involved in this process was sobering, not only between us and Southern Health, but also between senior and frontline staff. For example, senior staff insisted on being interviewed by Verita with lawyers present, while frontline staff were not afforded this layer of protection.

On 23 February 2014, George wrote a long email outlining her thoughts about how to move the campaign forward. It included this reflection:

Tomorrow

My hunch is that the slopey-shouldered cowards won't publish the report until as late as possible in the day tomorrow. I suggest that we let it sit, don't give too many (or any) teasers and just let everyone feel that sick to the pit of your stomach feeling as you wait for bad news.

George was right. There was anticipation on Twitter first thing Monday morning as people waited for the report to be published. As the hours passed, more Twitter interest was generated. By late afternoon it was clear that Southern Health had, again, made an error in judgement. Delaying publication of the report was further, very public, evidence of the disregard they demonstrated towards Connor and, by extension, us.

The report was eventually published just after 6pm. Before the advent of social media, people would have pretty much gone home by 6pm, but Twitter doesn't close.

Outrage was generated by the incontrovertible evidence that a young man had been failed by an NHS Trust, despite initial claims he had died of natural causes. The report, together with the failings identified by the CQC inspection, painted a picture of an NHS unit bereft of leadership, the most basic of healthcare provision and an almost wanton carelessness around the lives, and deaths, of patients.

A devastating discovery

Southern Health insisted on redacting names and job titles in the Verita report to keep staff anonymous and to prevent future investigations being compromised by staff not wanting to be honest. We found this odd because relevant staff would be named, and possibly called to be witnesses, at Connor's inquest. It also made the report difficult to follow, particularly for anyone one step removed from the micro detail.

In a more cynical moment, it's hard not to think that, too often, the clear and righteous path to thorough, open and transparent scrutiny at an inquest is deflected by the steps taken in the lead up to achieving it. So, the redacted names remain out of the public domain. I'll leave you to reflect on this as I go on to describe how the legal processes unfolded.

The content of the report was shocking, though by this stage we were not surprised. Across the 60 or so pages, the report authors could only find one or two positive comments among the failings. Connor hadn't had a chance. The level of care was negligible. The report authors defined Connor's death as preventable because the Unit staff had both knowledge (that Connor was diagnosed with epilepsy) and opportunity (Connor's seizure on 19 May) *'to take steps to stop the incident from happening and did not do so'*.

There were 23 findings, including:

F1 We found no evidence that an epilepsy profile was completed when CS was admitted to the unit. This was a key omission.

F5 There was no comprehensive care plan to manage CS's epilepsy.

F8 Staff should have increased their vigilance and monitoring of CS after his suspected seizure. This was a missed opportunity.

F11 We found no documentary evidence after 3 June that CS was observed in the bath every 15 minutes.

F12 Three of the 17 members of the unit team received training updates in epileptic care between October 2010 and August 2013.

F19 The unit lacked clinical leadership.

It concluded that his death was preventable; that it was the outcome of a lack of epilepsy care and the overall care provided by the Unit.

As I read the report in familiar tears, one extract from the minutes of a meeting on 3 June 2013 made me pause. It described a discussion about Connor saying he'd 'remembered' biting his tongue. As mentioned above, the report is redacted, so below the Trust employees are described as S3 and S9, and Connor as CS:

There has been no sign of seizure activity. [S3] has spoken to the staff around the time of the suspected seizure. [CS] says he remembers that he bit his tongue as he was in a bad mood, so he remembers the biting and the pain – [S9] explained that this doesn't appear consistent with a seizure.

By this stage the documentation, records, email exchanges and minutes replayed across my eyelids like a remorseless and relentless ticker tape when I tried and failed to sleep. Experience gained through pretty much 18 years of negotiating, and trying to keep on top of, various appointments, reports, blows and pronouncements relating to Connor had seamlessly shifted to a post-death mastery of the micro detail of records, documentation and other minutiae that related to his time in the Unit and earlier.

I knew I had not read anything about Connor remembering that he bit his tongue in anger.

It turned out that, instead of full sets of minutes for some of the weekly team meetings, we had been sent 'notes'. The notes did not include reference to the tongue biting. Connor's seizure in May was being questioned and we had no idea. His statement, the boy who always denied he had epilepsy, was taken to be evidence that he had not had a seizure after all.

Later, during Connor's inquest, Paul Bowen QC was to gently try and tease out of staff who was best placed to understand or interpret what Connor said or did. Who knew Connor best, or even well? Staff on a shift pattern of four days on and four days off, or his family?

Dr Murphy, the consultant psychiatrist who originally prescribed Bonjela for his bitten tongue, refused to be drawn when asked:

'Who is the best person to know what it is Connor means when he says something?'

'That's a very general question and it depends on the circumstances and what is being said.'

We had no idea that Connor's seizure activity was dismissed in a meeting on 3 June 2013, four weeks before he died. Why the fuck would you rule out a seizure in a patient with diagnosed epilepsy? For what purpose? We had no idea that Dr Murphy agreed to reduce Connor's observations to hourly given there was 'no evidence' of any seizure activity.

I can barely type these words as I feel such incredulity, intense rage and deep sadness at the grotesque absurdity of these actions.

Gaining momentum and friends

In March 2014, Norman Lamb, who was then Minister of State for Community and Social Care, was a secret attendee at a 'social care curry night' in London organised by George Julian. This was a local networking and social event for those who love curry and social care.

She asked me and Rich along so we could nobble him for a chat. We met in a pub earlier, the first time we had actually met George in person, which was odd given our interactions on Twitter and our already intense virtual campaign activity. We had a chuckle beforehand about how we might not get on with each other in person, but it was 'duck to water' stuff as soon as we met. She was just as I imagined: warm, bright, exuberant, funny and down to earth, with a cracking commitment to social justice.

Norman Lamb was seated at a separate table in the restaurant next to Richard Humphries, Senior Fellow in Social Care at The King's Fund. Time passed and it seemed we wouldn't get a chance to speak as a rumour circulated that Norman was about to leave. Rich disappeared and somehow sorted a spare seat next to him. By this time, I'd had a couple of pints and was pretty flustered and stressed. I sat down, took a deep breath and briefly summarised what had happened. After initial confusion, Norman Lamb became focused and concerned, and said he would follow it up. He did, and remains my favourite politician – kind and passionate, with a shedload of integrity and expertise.

He has regularly spoken up about Connor and Southern Health on local and national news and subsequently met with us to find out how progress was going with trying to gain accountability. He was pivotal in getting the Health and Safety Executive (HSE) to investigate Connor's death after writing to Richard Judge, CEO, and following this up with a meeting with the lead investigators some months later.

Around the same time, in desperation at no apparent action during the weeks following the publication of the Verita report, I tweeted David Nicholson, then CEO of NHS England, who agreed to meet with me and Rich – social media again proving to be a useful and levelling mechanism. Later, via a Freedom of Information request, we received the briefing document Southern Health produced for Nicholson ahead of this meeting. Another liberal dose of mother-blaming:

> To date, Ms Ryan has declined all invitations to meet with the Trust Chief Executive.
>
> The Trust has responded positively to media requests and more importantly it remains keen to engage properly with Connor's mother, Sara Ryan, but to date she has declined to meet with the Trust.
>
> Sadly, since the publication of the independent report the Trust has been subject to trolling on Twitter, a number of staff have been directly targeted and have felt intimidated by the

Twitter traffic. We are aware of at least one staff member's account having been hacked and a bogus Trust Twitter account has been set up.

We should be clear that there is absolutely no evidence that Sara Ryan is personally responsible for this trolling, hacking or intimidation but there are clearly some people who wish to use this case inappropriately.

There is a level of absurdity as well as offensiveness about this briefing which these extracts highlight. For several months, there were repeated requests for me and Rich to meet with Katrina Percy, the Chief Executive of Southern Health, from both the Southern Health executive board and wider, but it was never made clear to us what the point of such a meeting was, or why it would be useful. We said no to the original request because we both felt that the risk of us feeling worse during and after a meeting with her outweighed anything that could possibly be gained.

This briefing document sent to David Nicholson had a redacted but, again, clearly wide circulation list and there was no apparent dissent or objection to its content. If anyone in senior public service is reading this book, we can only ask that you engage in critical scrutiny and reflection in the communications you are party to or involved in, and keep at the forefront of your mind that a person has died and a family must be bereft. There is almost a childishness about these communications that should have generated some concern among the NHS England and other senior bods who received them.

As it was, despite – or perhaps because of – this document, the meeting with Nicholson, attended by Rich and me and Jane Cummings, Chief Nursing Officer, on 14 March 2014, was productive and efficient. The evening before we went, Rich suggested we ought to have some aims about what we were actually trying to achieve that we could put to David Nicholson, rather than just rehashing what had happened.

We banged out 'The Connor Manifesto' – a document laying out clearly what we wanted to see done in relation to what happened to Connor, but also for other learning-disabled people in NHS care – in the space of an hour and presented it to him at the meeting. You can read a copy in Appendix A.

A week or so before his retirement on 1 April 2014, he agreed to one of the main points listed:

To commission an investigation into the death of all patients with mental ill health or learning disabilities between 2011 (when Southern Health gained Foundation Trust status) and 2015.

This investigation was to become known as the Mazars review.

107 days of action

Following the misery of the findings of the Verita report, there arose a flickering light that was to become something incredibly important and special. A remarkable sense of collectivity and generosity was generated by those rallying against what had happened to Connor and the subsequent actions of Southern Health.

For example, early on, when we learned that legal representation for Connor's inquest would cost around £20,000, we began fundraising. This started as flogging some bits on eBay, including items donated by friends, and using the money raised to print postcards of Connor's artwork. We started selling these for £1 a pop on a fundraising blog. My mum volunteered to take responsibility for the orders, packaging and trips to the local post office, which she did using her legendary organisational skills. These baby steps grew into an unusually brilliant fundraising and awareness-raising effort.

Through growing support and interest on Twitter, awareness of the 107 days Connor spent in the Unit a year earlier grew. Just weeks after the Verita report was published, we launched a campaign, called #107daysofaction, to coincide with the first anniversary of Connor's admission to the Unit in which he spent the last 107 days of his life.

We asked people to adopt one of these 107 days to raise awareness, fundraise or do whatever they wanted to do.

There were no rules and little planning other than matching empty days to people asking to adopt them, and setting up a new website, #107daysofaction (https://107 daysofaction.wordpress.com). We asked people to share a few words about why they wanted to adopt the day and to focus on the positive. It was an organic punt with a back-up plan, as George and I were confident we could rehash existing posts from mydaftlife to fill each day if necessary.

This loosely organised happening on social media kicked off with us inviting people to send in postcards of 'awesome' telling us about what is fab about themselves. This set the scene for a flowering of a wonderful range and breadth of offerings we never imagined.

Some people volunteered to do something each day, such as a tweet about experiences of services, or a daily blog post reflecting on the experiences of being a teacher in the 1960s. People fundraised through donations in lieu of christening presents, a party night in two separate parts of Oxfordshire, cake sales, busking and other social events. Various merchandise items were produced, adding LB bus pencil cases, LB chocolates, notebooks and plants to the postcards and prints of Connor's artwork we'd started to sell. A young man called Jack made figures of cats from carefully recycled material.

There were blog posts; academic presentations and lectures; a balloon launch; an animation by David Harling called 'Far Beyond the Pale' (which you can watch on YouTube here: www.youtube.com/watch?v=gBmvfDqxOvw); an EP; a hair competition; a performance dedicated to Connor by comedians John Williams and King Cnut; and various sporting activities including 15-year-old Madi Barnicoat who canoed over 100 miles to the House of Commons with a photo of Connor on her back.

A letter, signed by 600 people, was published in *The Guardian* on 12 June 2014:

On the day of a House of Lords debate into the premature deaths of people with learning disabilities, we would like to highlight that support for people with learning disabilities and/or autism and their families should have four basic principles:

1) We should support people to live long, healthy, fulfilling and meaningful lives.

2) A learning disability and/or autism is not a health problem. Any additional health problems should be taken seriously and we should make sure that our health services work just as well for everyone who uses them.

3) We should respect, value and work closely with families and others who care about the person.

4) We should make sure that commissioners and providers are using the best available evidence to make decisions.

A meeting was held at the House of Commons, there were sponsored bus rides and bus drawings, and we ended up producing a Private Members Bill, the #LBBill, to try to change the law around the 'placing' of learning-disabled people in different settings.[2] One family of disability studies activists, the Lawthom-Goodleys, took a #JusticeforLB flag to Glastonbury and managed to get it featured on the front page of the BBC coverage of the festival. When the flag pole unexpectedly broke, they and their kids and friends picked up the flag and shared numerous pictures holding it up in various colourful, joy-filled and sometimes muddy settings. It was simply extraordinary.

Here are just a few examples of days chosen and why people wanted to be involved:

---

2   Norman Lamb supported the #LBBill and subsequently invited us to work with him on his Green Paper: *No voice unheard, no right ignored – a consultation for people with learning disabilities, autism and mental health conditions.*

Day 0, *The Guardian*

The first day, which began on 19 March 2014, was marked by a full two-page spread published in *The Guardian's* 'Society' pages. Written by journalist Saba Salman who has a learning-disabled sister, the piece was a hard-hitting account of what had happened to Connor and of our family's experiences, as well as providing a broader analysis of the experiences and treatment of learning-disabled people in the UK. The piece included extracts from my blog as well as a beautiful photo taken of Connor after a family day out and long walk on Hergest Ridge which runs along the border of Powys and Herefordshire – the photograph that features on the front cover of this book. He squats on his haunches, arms wrapped around his knees, wearing his favourite pale blue shirt with the sleeves carefully rolled up, looking the picture of contentment against a backdrop of early-summer-green brilliance.

Day 7, Sukey Carder

Sukey wrote:

I'm competing in a charity hair show in Corby, Northants, to raise money for The Epilepsy Society and Dreams Come True. So far, we're up to £800 and still counting! I am using LB's postcard as my inspiration for one of my models, as I wanted to use this event to not only raise money for an epilepsy charity but to raise awareness too. It will be quite a big event [with the] Mayor, principal of the college, press etc., but most of all it will be joyous, with singers and highland dancers!

I first 'met' Sara when a mutual acquaintance asked people to send her some support as her son, LB, had gone into Slade House [the STATT Unit], and she was struggling. Thus a little support network sprang up, a little nod here and there, hello, thinking of you, keep smiling, don't worry, one mother to another, why wouldn't you? Imagine, well, you don't need to imagine, my horror after coming home after a great night out for my wedding anniversary, to find a distraught Sara saying LB had died. I decided that however much or little I could do to support her, I would.

I am honoured to support the campaign/movement Justice for LB and so pleased that this charity fundraiser coincides with 107days.

Day 9, Fiona Fisher, parent carer

Fiona wrote:

I first 'met' Sara and LB on Twitter in 2012 and we soon chatted passionately and amicably about our common loves and hates about being mums to incredible dudes with additional needs. I remember in particular a conversation about filling out the ludicrous Department for Work and Pensions form to apply for Employment and Support Allowance… 'Can you pick up a pen?' 'Can you set an alarm clock?' It was another instance of proving inability to the authorities that we've been doing since the get go…and it was a relief to talk/rant with Sara because she understood my exasperation exactly.

I won't go into detail about the #JusticeforLB campaign here. I feel utterly inadequate to the task of capturing anything but the tiniest flavour of horror, outrage and disgust that LB died a preventable death…but there's also the feeling of tenacity, forensic analysis and solidarity among the #JusticeforLB posse.

Day 14, Dr Damian Milton

It was in 2007 that I first interviewed Damian Milton for an autism research project. Damian, a mature student at the time, was autistic and had a young autistic son. I remember turning up at his flat in Kent with my video camera, tripod and interview schedule. By that time, I'd probably interviewed around 20 autistic adults and parents of autistic kids and, in each interview, I was learning more about autism. The interview with Damian added to this learning. By 2014, this thoughtful and intensely bright man was a doctoral student and a key figure in the autistic community in the UK. He adopted Day 14 in celebration of World Autism Awareness Day and wrote a blog post called Moments in Time, which included this extract:

> Around the world today, autistic people and especially those who are less verbal or are deemed 'learning disabled' are dehumanised, incarcerated, restrained, bullied, therapised, normalised, neglected, and I could carry on and on, with such a list. What leads to this abuse of those divergent from the normative ideal? What leads to 'death by indifference'? How is one meant to find Justice for LB and all the young (and older) 'dudes' (of whatever gender orientation)? This is something I (and many others) would like the world to think about today, the 14th day of the #107days campaign.

Damian went on to talk about his experiences of growing up, his experiences of academia and his developing (brilliant) academic career, and the autistic community. He said:

> Since then, I have gone on to present about autism over 70 times at various events and conferences, I have had a number of articles published, and I have a paid job as a consultant for

the National Autistic Society's 'Ask autism' project. In order for autistic people to be confident to do such things, we need our allies. I felt that Sara was one of my first in the field.

This was early days in terms of the (known about) mother-blaming and battering that was to ensue, and it was a tonic to read.

Day 27, Anne-Marie Boylan and Louise Locock

Anne-Marie and Louise wrote:

Today and tomorrow we are singing in the mediaeval chapel of Bartlemas in Oxford. We are singing music for Lent, especially Lamentations by various composers. The Lamentations are a collection of poetic laments for the destruction of Jerusalem, supposedly written by the Prophet Jeremiah. They are a cry of undeserved pain, songs of irretrievable disaster, bitterness, suffering and grief. That seemed all too appropriate for Justice for LB, whatever your religious views.

What's even more poignant in this case is the setting. Bartlemas Chapel was part of a medieval leper colony. Lepers, of course, have traditionally been seen as being on the margins of society, feared, misunderstood and isolated – the very word 'leper' came to mean anyone who was an outcast. Monks set up the colony at Bartlemas outside the city walls to care for them, both physically and spiritually – and recent scholarship has suggested we may need to change our views about how lepers were seen and treated. A report from community excavations at Bartlemas says:

What the archaeological evidence provides is an emerging picture of lepers not as outcasts, but as members integrated into the social fabric of medieval society and treated with some measure of dignity and respect.

Maybe those monks could teach Southern Health a thing or two?

Day 40, @Ermintrude2, social worker and blogger on social care and health policy

@Ermintrude2 wrote:

I wanted to write something to remember and honour LB, his family and people who are in similar situations now. I wanted to rage against systems that allowed this to happen but as I've read people's contributions, I realise I can't add more honesty than those who have experienced the utter despair and despicable treatment in the hands of health and social care professionals. So I am just pondering some memories, fitting them together and thinking about what I can do to promote better care and better systems for people who have learning disabilities and for all people who are subject to the vagaries of a disjointed and unempathetic system.

Day 83, Alicia Wood, Housing and Support Alliance

Alicia wrote:

Housing and Support Alliance is supporting #JusticeforLB because Connor and his family only wanted something simple and straightforward – to get the help they needed and had a right to in difficult times – and it ended in the most unimaginable tragedy. We know that people with learning disabilities who have the most complicated needs can and do get good help, a good place to live and the support they need to live there. It is doable and affordable, yet all over the country there are still many people with learning disabilities and families getting poor and mediocre support, being sent away from the people they love because there is no decent support locally and being needlessly hospitalised when all they need is for professionals to listen and respond. It is an outrage.

Each contribution was, in its own way, magical – I've included a full list of events and contributors at the back of this book (see Appendix B). It was as if the format – no fuss, no pressure, just do something – gave people the freedom and confidence to step up and get involved.

People clearly thought carefully about what they could do, often referencing Connor's enthusiasms which they had come to know through my blog. London buses regularly featured, and a group of mothers arranged a day trip to Connor's favourite bus museum.

Some even helped to achieve Connor's dreams: Rodgers Coaches in Northampton and Earthline, a heavy haulage company in Wiltshire, named two double-decker red school buses and a Scania truck respectively after him.

The magic spread abroad as one supporter adopted a day to stick notes about the campaign on bus stops in the town she lived in in France; a New Zealand group of Brownies drew buses in chalk on the playground; and Mark Sherry, an Australian academic at the University of Toledo, Ohio, produced a short film with his students and their families in support of the campaign. Anne Townsend, a medical sociologist living in Vancouver, committed to photographing and tweeting a bus with a postcard of Connor's bus picture each day. It was such a treat to look forward to her daily photo.

Our back-up plan of rehashing blog posts was not needed, as towards the last few weeks of the 107 days we ended up doubling or even tripling the target for adopters of days. George adopted a day for a sponsored head-shave towards the end, which raised £5000 to be shared between the campaign and the hospice where her dad had died a few years earlier.

The campaign was an unexpected but much-welcomed distraction across that period, countering the constant companions of despair, blackness and heartbreak. We left Day 107, the first anniversary of Connor's death on 4 July 2014, unplanned as we couldn't bear to think about it. In the end, we suggested that people changed their Twitter profile photos to a black and white picture of Connor in a white shirt and jacket at his school prom to mark the day (the photo which features on page 30).

We spent that day at home with family and friends. I dipped into Twitter a few times as my iPad beeped constant notifications; it was astonishing to see Connor's photo spread across my timeline. When I eventually fell into bed in the early hours of the morning, beyond sad, drunk and exhausted, I couldn't believe the support for the final day of the campaign.

The band Divine Comedy had even tweeted us…

The Divine Comedy
@divinecomedyhq

Replying to @JusticeforLB

@JusticeforLB Wishing you all the best, love DCHQ x #107days #justiceforLB

RETWEETS 25 LIKES 21

9:24 AM - 4 Jul 2014

Their song, *National Express*, had become the unofficial campaign anthem.

Your inquest was nearly two years ago now. You would have found it fascinating.

Mum, was there a judge, Mum?

There was a Coroner. A type of judge (I think). It was held in County Hall. Just through the canteen, which was weird. You had a jury.

How many people on the jury, Mum?

Nine. And eight legal teams with barristers and solicitors. Yours was the best by far.

Barristers, Mum? Were there barristers, Mum?

Yep.

Mum? Did people give evidence, Mum?

Yep. Lots of people gave evidence.

Did they swear an oath, Mum?

Yep, everyone had to swear an oath.

On a Bible, Mum?

Well, a Bible or some sort of affirmation statement thing.

Mum? What did the Coroner say, Mum?

He was sorry you died.

CHAPTER 7

The Waiting Game

There is particular pain associated with the preventable death of a loved one in the care of the NHS. First, the shock associated with finding out that the organisation which you have grown up thinking of only in terms of benevolent goodness can act with malevolence. This realisation involves the peeling back of layers of awfulness over time as more details are uncovered or further brutality is meted out to the family by the Trust.

Second, because this catastrophic happening occurred within such a monolithic institution, there is an unremitting, unchecked, almost wanton drawing out of never quite pinning down what happened. Every step takes so much longer than can be humanly possible. You are typically the last to know any tiny development or decision. Documents are circulated to you at least a week or so after other relevant people, the Trust, local authority or broader, receive them. Decisions are eventually relayed to you as an afterthought or when you chase them up.

Families are consigned to harsh and liminal spaces, unable to grieve effectively for their loved ones and always waiting for the next disclosure, revelation or step in the process. These invariably happen late on a Friday afternoon or Saturday morning when there is no one to have recourse to, to ask for clarification, to rage at or simply respond to. We can only think that this delay is an effective mechanism for eventually closing down family quests for accountability and may even be actively pursued as a way of managing family protest into oblivion.

At the same time, there is no one person or organisation to turn to, to say, 'Help. Can you please do something?'

In the early days after Connor died, I would end my blog posts regularly appealing to someone to step up and do something. As time passed with tumbleweed-type non-responses, I got more grandiose and ridiculous in these pleas, requests, demands...the Pope, some sort of divine deity. It was a complete waste of time. There is no one. The system is fucked.

On a vaguely related note, while access to social media gives sidelined families a platform, I can't help thinking that some of the skills derived from my training as an academic have helped during the campaign – research skills including analysis, reflection and critical engagement contribute to effective campaigning.

Academic training provided some tools to enable me, Rich and others to just about hold a steady course through the shite, while trying to maintain clear and measured pressure on those responsible.

One bit of action was the review agreed by David Nicholson into the deaths within the Southern Health learning disability and mental health services. This was awarded to accountancy firm Mazars and was led by Mary-Ann Bruce, a woman who would demonstrate immoveable integrity, knowledge, strength and decency across the course of the review.

In December 2014 we agreed to be on the steering group and were invited to meet the Mazars team and a representative from Thames Valley NHS England at an introductory meeting held at Oxford Brookes University. We pitched up, both of us with a bit of a buzz of anticipation that some kick-ass action was starting. Within minutes we found out that a representative from Southern Health was already on the steering group. Rich, in particular, was furious; he stormed out of the meeting, returning briefly to reiterate his utter frustration and anger.

The meeting finished shortly after this.

By this stage, we'd experienced repeated examples of Southern Health having insider knowledge and power over what was to happen. To find out that this new review, ostensibly independently commissioned by NHS England, already had the Trust on board and involved was baffling.

There was a sharpish backtracking on the composition of the steering group. Southern Health were off the gig and two 'lay' members would be involved in place of Rich and me: George Julian selected by us, and Bill Love[1] by NHS England. It was an inauspicious start to a review which was to subsequently become an exempler in how to independently review a public sector organisation.

Meanwhile, my niece Ally Rogers analysed four Southern Health documents for her undergraduate dissertation in

---

1   Head of Development and Support Training at NDTi (National Development Team for Inclusion) by NHS England.

linguistics at Leeds University. She included a remarkable letter Katrina Percy wrote to me, littered with 'I am absolutely right…' statements. Ally concluded:

> *I only looked at four texts so it's not really possible to make sweeping statements about Southern Health based on these findings but in these texts there appears to be some deliberate manipulation by Southern Health and its staff in assigning blame and taking credit for actions, as well as intentional avoidance of producing an actual apology and risking admitting responsibility for negative actions.*
>
> *The division between 'good' Southern Health and 'bad' staff is interesting as it shows a lack of 'duty of care to staff', something that they emphasise throughout the communications. The findings also contradict the NHS 'Being Open' policy that is designed to avoid shady communications, which suggests that this kind of communication isn't widespread across the NHS and that Southern Health needs a reminder.*
>
> *So, what now? As satisfying as it is to know that I managed to use my degree to give a giant middle finger to Katrina Percy et al., realistically I'm just an undergraduate with a long essay to wave at Southern Health. What would be ace is if someone who could use these findings for positive change (i.e. someone from Southern Health who reads this), actually had the balls to admit that their communications could do with a bit more openness.*

Unsurprisingly, Ally's wish didn't materialise.[2]

---

2 Ally went on to do her Master's dissertation focusing on apologies in the NHS – one of many examples where Connor's death has had an impact on the direction of people's lives and the choices they make.

Brilliant things were happening alongside the delay, prevarication and worse. The North West Regional Forum of people with learning disabilities marked #JusticeforLB at their annual conference with a powerful, silent holding up of #JusticeforLB signs after playing the latest animation from David Harling, 'In Search of Rights and Colour' (www.youtube.com/watch?v=UKVXc1am5BM).

The Ohio-based academic Mark Sherry continued his campaign in the USA and put forward a motion to the Society for the Study of Social Problems stating that what happened to Connor would be discussed at the next annual conference in Chicago. The motion was passed unanimously.

Further robust and heartfelt responses outside the UK to what had happened to Connor involved disability studies academics and activists, Katherine Runswick-Cole and Dan Goodley, taking the #JusticeforLB flag (that his family had enthusiastically and passionately waved at Glastonbury in 2014 and 2015) to Australia and New Zealand, meeting self-advocacy groups, the Disability Commissioner for New Zealand and various academic and activist audiences.

Death anniversaries

Death anniversaries involve a terrible dread, threatening an always fragile, post-death 'new' life. The D-day itself is awful and has brutally trumped Connor's birthday. It's only as the day draws to an end and I can slope off to bed, numbed with beer, wine and the love and support of family and friends, that there is a slight release. This is repeated with birthdays, which have a different pain structure, and other celebrations like Christmas and Easter.

On Connor's 19th birthday in November 2013 – the first since his death – we organised a party at the Oxfordshire Bus Museum he loved. It is a small museum with working buses which only opens on Wednesdays and Saturdays. The museum trustee board demonstrated such care and earnestness in arranging this on a Sunday. My mum and older sister Tracey, also known as 'Agent T' of Team LB, would run the canteen serving tea and cake while museum staff would open up the museum buildings and lay on a vintage bus ride at 3pm. There was a great turnout.

We huddled in the canteen with our mugs of tea while people wandered round the different museum buildings, enjoying the exhibits: buses, well-dressed mannequins, stuffed animals and bus memorabilia. The bus ride replicated one I'd done with Connor on a trip out of the Unit.

The next year, on Connor's 20th birthday, Rosie, Owen and I went to the Tower of London in memory of the infamous 'failed' trip. We visited at the tail end of a breathtaking installation of 888,246 hand-made poppies at the Tower by Paul Cummins and Tom Piper – each representing the death of a British and Commonwealth soldier during World War One. We had lunch in the restaurant in the wall of the Tower and, after wandering around, we blitzed bus-related stuff in the Tower shop, even buying a London bus tie for Rich to wear to Connor's inquest.

That first Christmas, I couldn't stomach any thought of festivities and on Christmas Eve dragged the kids and Rich to some backend-of-beyond budget hotel in Barcelona for a few days. We've slowly rebuilt Christmas. Rich has replaced the tree decorations, carefully packing those gut-wrenching hand-made decorations away in the loft – the ones from nursery and primary school years that made us chuckle every year when we rediscovered them. Most notable among them was the 'Baby Cheesus', a gold spray-painted walnut with a squidge of cotton wool stuck to it. This year I helped decorate the tree again. 'Progress' that I appreciate.

Writing this four years after Connor's death, I can say the pain becomes less obliterating of daily life. It doesn't go away, but it can be gently eased to one side or even parked out of sight for periods of time – sometimes not deliberately, which is good. Our house is full of Connor's paintings, photos and the brilliance generated through the campaign: the cross-stitch double-decker bus with Chunky Stan as a passenger made by my 'life-raft' mate Becca above my computer in the back room; the exquisitely embroidered photo of Connor by the artist Maurizio Anzeri[3] on the wall behind me; the intricate textile artwork Janet Read started on the train to Oxford on the day of Connor's funeral, *A Landscape for a Sparrowhawk*, in the front room. Janet is a force for good in the social care world, Emeritus Professor at Warwick University and my much-loved PhD supervisor.

Bus-related memorabilia is still scattered around the house, on shelves, catching the sunshine through stained glass or carried around by me every day. The fridge has photos of Connor making his first cup of tea at school and eating a pasty at the farm. The colour painting we used on fundraising postcards is at the top of the stairs, and everywhere there are boxes, pictures, trinkets and nightlight holders Connor painted, made or stuck stuff to.

I still wear his navy blue cardy at home. For the first few months after he died, I slept with the few of his unwashed

---

3   Maurizio, an artist friend of Alicia Wood who embroiders vintage photos, said he would embroider a photo of Connor after Alicia told him what had happened (www.saatchigallery.com/artists/maurizio_anzeri.htm).

t-shirts we found.[4] I was desperate to hold onto his smell and asked a friend whose husband had died a few years before about how to do this. The holding onto the few bits there were, and regret and sadness about not having advance warning to prepare what I wanted (while knowing it would never be enough), remains impossible to make sense of. A clipping of his rock star locks. More video footage. The beauty of his laughter in a bottle. Him.

A wooden chest in our room, currently under a pile of clothes, contains treasures we carefully selected and packed during that baking hot summer in 2013. Friends decanted Connor's stuff from his room, carefully packing everything, including apparent rubbish, into bags and bags and bags for life. Rosie and I sorted through these bags over that summer. Laughing and crying, flicking through notebooks containing repeated stick man drawings of Tom Chaplin from the band Keane, people with guns, and 'Connor rocks!', 'London rocks!' and 'Buses rock!', written in large letters in fluorescent markers on page after page of small, lined notebooks. Everything we took out of those bags just spoke to the life of a quirky and unusual dude who filled his days with the stuff he loved.

Every crumb of detritus was examined and sorted into 'chest', 'loft', 'charity shop' and 'rubbish' in true 'life laundry' style. The pouch of mermaid shells turned up too late to be buried with Connor. He wore his Sebastian Bonaparte t-shirt, his mechanics overalls, the trainers we'd only bought for him weeks earlier, with his beloved first aid book, a couple of buses, some septic tank pages torn out of *Yellow Pages*

---

4   The Unit, somewhat ironically, seemed to wash clothes obsessively and his boiled and shrunken garments were returned with some that didn't belong to him.

and photos. The funeral home crossed his arms across his chest and tucked a photo of me in one of his hands.

A spontaneous act of anti-mother-blame.

I wrote this on my blog on 29 August 2013:

Eight weeks on

Bit of a tough 24 hours really. Starting with an unannounced, unexpected lengthy weep fest yesterday evening, sitting in the armchair upstairs. I'm not sure I was even crying really. Well not in any way I've ever experienced before. And boy, we are talking some serious crying in the last two months. This was a serious case of tumbling tears. So plentiful I had to move LB's smelly t-shirt out of the way to avoid slushing the smells out of it. That action, in itself, increased the tear flow. My low-level, constant concern about the dilution or disappearance of the smells. The lynx deodorant smells have almost gone (but can be topped up I suppose, although this seems a bit like faking it, so I'll keep the two separate for now). But LB's body eau-der is clinging on. Valiantly. Love him. He had so many employment options open to him, if life wasn't so fucking stacked against any recognition of these dudes' talents, abilities and strengths. I've always thought this.

I wonder if the extreme crying was sparked by the first iteration of chest sorting. A slow recognition that there would be little new stuff to add. No new notebooks to enjoy and marvel at. No new 'Pupil of the Week' sheets. Yawning spaces ahead. For all of us. Life without LB. What does that mean? How can we possibly make any sense of it? Especially when we all miss him so fucking much.

Today was slightly better. In the sense that the tear downpour had dried to an intermittent drizzle. Not brilliant though. I did

the weekly countdown type thing to his death this morning.
Again, completely unhelpful and crushingly painful, as it has
been for each of the past eight weeks. I continue to gasp for air
regularly as the reality of what has happened stamps on my
throat. Bastard grief.

Bastard Unit. Bastard health 'care'. Bastard social 'care'.

I messed around kind of aimlessly later this afternoon
trying to organise LB's bus collection into something I could
capture on camera. The third attempt in the past two months.
This one as unsuccessful as the others. This is bugging me as
his bus collection was so important to him. I piled the models
back into the box and thought about the crap pictures I'd taken.

I browsed back through the thousands of photos I have.
Relentless snapper I am. It suddenly became important, in
much the same way that I'm laying down markers for various
'last things', 'when did that happen', 'in what order was x, y
or z' (as I persistently bug Rich with), to find the very last
photo I took of LB. What a terrible marker. Such complete
sadness. All over again.

The room-dismantling was a labour of love and loss
undertaken with remarkable care and respect by friends. I
know some people can't bear to touch the bedroom of a
child who dies, something I can so understand. I can only
think it becomes harder to do later. On the few occasions
I've opened Connor's chest of treasures in our bedroom, I
can barely breathe – the pain is dizzyingly, and dazzlingly,
unbearable.

PART IV

THE INQUEST

CHAPTER 8

A Very Adversarial Affair

Following a report of a death, the State Coroner must decide if it is necessary to hold an inquest to determine the cause and circumstances of the death. The inquest is a key moment or event in finding out how and why someone died and an essential step in gaining justice. The coronial process, as we were to find out, is an intricate, archaic, law-drenched and uncertain journey in which families without expert legal representation are too easily silenced.

The state had an operational duty to protect Connor's life because he was in the Unit and, because this duty was breached, he was entitled to an 'Article 2' inquest – a more thorough examination of what happened. Article 2 inquests can involve a jury.

There were four pre-inquest review meetings between November 2014 and Connor's inquest which began on 5 October 2015. These two-hour meetings, held in the Coroner's Court, were to thrash out the shape and size of the inquest.

I write this section drawing on what we learned from our legal advisors Caoilfhionn Gallagher, Charlotte Haworth Hird and Selen Cavcav from INQUEST in the days after Connor died. We would not have known what an Article 2 inquest was if it bopped us on the head before 2013. I joke, but this is a serious issue.

Families typically don't know about coronial processes. 'Not knowing what you don't know' was a frequent backdrop to Connor's childhood, as it was through interactions with mates and other families with disabled children when that crucial detail was typically gained. Without the representation of solicitors and barristers with relevant, human rights expertise, families are completely disempowered within this process. Our 'team' now included:

- Caoilfhionn Gallagher, a ferociously committed and fearless barrister (now QC) with tireless energy, expertise and compassion.

- Charlotte Haworth Hird, a thoughtful, meticulous, sharp and brilliant solicitor who was reassuring and deeply sensitive.

- Paul Bowen, an experienced and knowledgeable Queen's Counsel with a keenly analytical mind and the ability to cut to the chase with an unusual immediacy.

- Keina Yoshida, Caoilfhionn's new pupil who, again, was reassuring with her strong commitment to human rights issues and intellect.

They were also warm and engaging with a sense of humour – desirable criteria after the essential expertise boxes are ticked. The dude had the very best fighting his corner.

It was bleedingly obvious that, without this team and the support of INQUEST, we would have made no inroads into the impenetrable wall of protection that exists around public sector organisations. We would have naively assumed that the Coroner was going to carefully examine all the evidence and determine how Connor died and why.

In reality this assumption is founded on a belief that a Trust, or other public sector body, is willing to act with candour and integrity and will actually want to find out exactly what happened. 'Dream on sunshine' is my response to this assumption.

Our residual naivety was crushed at the first pre-inquest review meeting when, despite having publicly accepted the findings of the Verita investigation in February 2014, Southern Health appeared to have turned up determined to resist the case for an Article 2 inquest and for a jury. They circulated their legal submission late, just before the meeting started. It was a lengthy legal document of dense case law and arguments. The content left us stunned.

The Trust argued that the operational obligation to fully investigate Connor's death was met by the various ongoing investigations, including those by the police, the Health and Safety Executive, NHS England and the CQC. This, they argued, meant an Article 2 inquest was not necessary. (Connor was entitled to an Article 2 inquest because the State breached their duty of care to him and he died.)

Their argument around a jury was even more staggering. Two conditions have to be met in order for a jury to be empanelled. I'm reproducing the following extracts verbatim from their submission because it's probably useful to get an idea of how family members are discussed in these settings, and the level of legal expertise families can face within the inquest process.

> *The first is the deceased dying in State detention, the second is that:*
>
> *(i) the death was a violent or unnatural one, or*
>
> *(ii) the cause of death is unknown.*

While accepting that Connor died in state detention, the submission stated that Connor's death was not violent or unnatural and the cause was not unknown. It was drowning as a result of an epileptic seizure.

> *28. In the premises it is submitted that this was not an unnatural death and that the mandatory requirements for empanelling a jury cannot be met.*

The Trust was actually arguing that death by drowning is a natural way to die. Connor drowned in a hospital bath. When I think of him not waving back at me from the car outside Somerfield, of his consistently subtle resistance to the nonsensical expectations of acceptable and normative behaviour, and his unwavering belief in social justice, and contrast this to the brutal contempt with which his adult life and death was treated, I felt, and still feel, utter sadness.

The submission continued:

> *29. HM Coroner retains a discretion to do so where he thinks 'there is sufficient reason to do so'. The Trust of course*

acknowledges that the family's views are an important consideration, but they are not wholly determinate of the matter.

30. HM Coroner can reassure the family that an Inquest conducted by him will be no less fearless, independent or thorough.

Two further points exemplifying the gamesmanship and inhumanity of the process: a rallying call to the Coroner's fearlessness and independence, and a subtle putting of us, 'the family', in our place. The level of power-wielding and obliterating of humanity in a context of apparent public service is simply extraordinary. The strength of the fight we clearly had with the Trust was laid bare during that meeting.

Securing a jury

Sitting on the hard, wooden benches of the courtroom and listening to this should have been a warning for what was to come during the inquest, but we were too focused on getting an Article 2 inquest and jury agreed to think about what lay ahead. These additional layers of scrutiny were essential to finding out what had happened and a step towards accountability for Connor's death.

This hearing made nonsense of the argument that inquests are 'inquisitorial rather than adversarial'. Around that time on the Radio 4 *You and Yours* programme (14 January 2015), the then Minister for Justice and Civil Liberties, Simon Hughes, argued, with reference to another young man who died shortly before Southern Health took

over Oxfordshire services, that families did not need legal aid
to cover representation at inquests:

> An inquest is aimed at helping families find out the
> circumstances behind the death of their loved one. Lawyers are
> not usually required, as the hearings are specifically designed
> so people without legal knowledge can easily participate
> and understand what is happening. The Coroner is there to
> investigate the death and can put questions on behalf of the
> family during proceedings.

This statement, which is utter bollocks, demonstrates how
the Ministry of Justice colludes in ignoring the actions of
Trusts and other public bodies at inquests, or are ignorant
of them. Either position is unacceptable. From the moment
Connor died, it felt like a well-oiled machine, involving the
Southern Health in-house and external legal representatives,
was cementing a wall of denial. We couldn't meticulously use
case law to construct a strong argument that Connor should
have an Article 2 inquest, as our legal team were to do. And,
with respect to the quietly spoken and serious Coroner, he
didn't have the necessary understanding of Connor to do so
on our behalf.

As it was, the Coroner dismissed the 'drowning as natural
causes' argument immediately and, after much law-drenched
deliberation and discussion, agreed to an Article 2 inquest
before the second pre-inquest hearing. Elation and relief
was followed weeks later by despair. On 22 December 2014,
just in time for Christmas number two without Connor, the
Coroner wrote to say that he would not be calling a jury. His
rationale was that Connor was not 'in custody or otherwise
in state detention' and was free to leave the Unit.

This issue of the Unit not being a 'locked unit' was a red herring.[1] The Coroner repeatedly came back to the argument that, had Connor asked for the front door to be unlocked, the staff would have unlocked it. He therefore did not technically count as someone who was detained. That he would never ask for the door to be unlocked was irrelevant. He desperately wanted to leave the Unit and the staff knew that, to the extent that he had been told he would be able to go home sooner if he attended the emotions group each week.[2]

If the doors had been unlocked, he would not have left the Unit without us picking him up. He had never been out on his own.

He didn't open the door to me years earlier when I locked myself out.

In the event, at the second review hearing in January 2015, Paul Bowen effectively argued that Connor was detained and the Coroner eventually agreed to a jury.

It was already an exhausting and draining experience, and we were in a privileged position. Families without legal representation are in a precarious position, facing unlimited legal representation by the Trust, or other public sector body. Learning-disabled people who die unexpectedly without family are very unlikely to have their deaths properly investigated. They simply don't count.

As a bit of an aside, I wrote a letter to Simon Hughes about this, and he invited me to meet him in the House of Commons. He seemed to listen to what I was saying but

---

1   Southern Health agreed that Connor was detained, hence the argument of drowning as a natural cause of death.

2   At the time, this was presented to us as progress that Connor was making while in the Unit. We found out, through reading the records after he died, that he was coerced into attending.

remained resolute in his belief that the coronial process was not adversarial. He had an unswerving faith in the strength and integrity of Coroners to – fearlessly – manage the process of grief-stricken families on the one side and a well-armed stock of in-house and external lawyers and barristers on the part of the NHS Trust, with unlimited funds.

As an outcome of the Hillsborough inquest, the inequity of this process is now being strongly challenged and the Chief Coroner has called for legal aid to be provided to families. Perhaps sense will finally prevail.

The final pre-inquest hearing

The remaining two pre-inquest hearings focused on deciding who would give evidence in person or by statement, the timings and a myriad of other minutiae, like how to weed out jurors who were following my blog or the #JusticeforLB Twitter feed. Families have got in touch with us, in similar situations, saying they had been advised to not say anything publicly about what had happened before the inquest into their loved one's death. Paul, Caoilfhionn and Charlotte were happy for us to tweet and blog about the process and, I think, the public unfolding of this process was a core part of the support we received. Southern Health were exercised by this and wanted to make sure no #JusticeforLB supporters were on the jury.

John Lish, another member of Team LB, wrote a guest blog after attending the final pre-inquest hearing on the #JusticeforLB blog (http://justiceforlb.org/pre-inquest-review-meeting-no-4-justiceforlb), which I've reproduced in part here with his permission.

Let's consider three separate Southern Health barrister's arguments made during the hearing: about allowing Rich to give evidence; whether Sara should be allowed to give oral evidence twice;[3] and the argument about excluding jurors who have read the blogs about Connor. These for me have a common root. Namely, these are attempts to minimise the presence of Connor as a living and beloved young man with the jury.

Especially dangerous are the blogs and campaigns for Connor and their connection to the sense of wrong that this beloved young man was taken away from his family. A shared humanity and outrage.

The request by the Southern Health barrister that jurors be excluded with any knowledge of the case was part of this minimising process and was a bargaining position to influence the Coroner's questioning of potential jury members. The sheepish response to the Coroner's gently acerbic comment that it was going to be unlikely that any jury would be found under those conditions demonstrated that. The target was the exclusion of voices and opinions, especially Sara's.

It is in Southern Health's interest to minimise the human element, to make it a technical discussion about care plans and staff functions. Juries are known to be more sceptical of authorities or appeal to authority, so this jury presents problems for Southern Health.

This seems especially so, given how they presented new evidence to the Coroner as it feels clear that they are basing their arguments around the care plan written for Connor. The presenting of emails and the interrogated data of the care plan

---

3   The issue of my giving evidence twice was because the Coroner wanted an outline of what had happened at the beginning of the inquest, while our legal team said I should be able to give my evidence after the Southern Health staff had given their evidence.

do seem to demonstrate Southern Health strategy for the inquest itself. Essentially the inquest boils down to a simple equation: either the structures and systems that Southern Health had in place were insufficient, which places responsibility with the upper management of the Trust; or the care plan developed through those structures/systems was robust and it was a failure of staff to fulfil their roles.

Hence I think the exchange between the Southern Health barrister and the Coroner re the email evidence was significant, because of her insistence that these emails didn't constitute part of Connor's care plan. That raised a flag with me, as it separates the behaviour of staff from Southern Health systems. Equally, this new data from the care plan also feels, with reflection, to be an attempt to differentiate between the creation of the care plan and the implementation of said care plan. I wonder if any of the other interested parties have images of drawbridges being raised?

Obviously, there is a hierarchy of what Southern Health want to achieve in terms of a jury verdict, but the strategy feels clear having witnessed this pre-inquest hearing.

After two hours of legal discussions and with outstanding arguments still to be agreed through written correspondence with the Coroner, the hearing ended. Just another afternoon of toil for Sara and Richard, amongst many. The inquest will be hard, as it will be day upon day of discussing their son as an object for legal inquiry. My heart goes out to them.

I can only hope that the jury finds a connection to Connor, feels the same outrage that so many share about the casual dismissal of a life and demands that accountability is required.

The #JusticeforLB quilt – unifying experiences

After #107daysofaction, the campaign continued its focus on pushing for change, keeping a clear eye on Southern Health's actions and activities and generating magic.

Janet Read, Emeritus Professor at Warwick University, used the day she adopted (Day 59), along with two friends, Janis Firminger and Margaret Taylor, to ask people to produce patches measuring 10cm by 15cm with the intention of creating a #JusticeforLB quilt. As they wrote at the time:

> We have a vision of a large, strong, colourful, quite disorderly quilt or blanket that reflects the mood of the contributions people have been making through social media.
>
> The blog posts, tweets and the rest capture a lot of love, affection, fury, sharp insights, analysis, good politics, protest and decent humanity all unified around LB's story and the determination to get justice for him. That's the sort of quilt we'd like to make. A really good piece of 'outsider art', if you like. You don't have to think of yourself as an artist to take part, you just have to want to do it. Anyone, yes anyone, can join in.

Large, strong, colourful and quite disorderly – the essence of the campaign captured in a few words. Janet rented a PO box for a few weeks and the patches started to roll in. She later wrote:

> The hundreds of contributions we received were more arresting, inventive, moving, irreverent, colourful and thoughtful than anything we could have hoped for. They were mostly from the UK but other contributors lived in Japan, Romania, the USA, Canada, Morocco, France and Spain. Patches came embroidered, appliquéd, crayoned, painted, felt-tipped,

crocheted and knitted and were made by men, women and children whose ages ranged from three to eighty-five years. While many patches were from accomplished embroiderers, lots were by novices and had apologetic notes attached asking if they were good enough. Good enough? Every single one!

Many people sent stories or letters with their patches, which contributed to an even richer quilt as the meaning of some of the patches was made clear. For example, Kara wrote:

The quilt patch has a dark-brown background of material from a school-play costume I designed and made for Grenouille [Kara's child who has a rare genetic rearrangement]. I wanted Connor to have something linked to G. The design is an appliqué shamrock leaf in bright-green felt, comprising three separate leaves with the main veins delineated in silver lurex back-stitch embroidery, plus a stalk also embroidered in silver back-stitch: 'Kara xx'. The four felt pieces are individually stitched to the backing with silver lurex thread, using blanket stitch.

In the centre of the leaf is a large brilliant, also sewn on, with silver thread whip-stitch, for the 'Drops of Brilliance' post. As I said on that post, 'I wanted some brilliant raindrops, and I wanted them on a shamrock, partly because we have been so lucky with people willing to drop brilliance into G's life, partly because of the heart-shaped leaves, but mostly as a reminder of LB's love of Ireland.' I rather liked that the brilliant was originally from a chandelier, since the purpose of #107days is to shed light on the murk surrounding LB's death.

Finally, the words '107 days', for the time Connor spent held in STATT before dying there, were embroidered freehand onto the empty corner, using green cotton embroidery thread twisted with green and silver lurex. I started with stem stitch for the '107' but found it didn't work particularly well on the textured background material so used chain stitch for the 'days'. I wished I had done chain stitch from the beginning, as on reflection it was a much more appropriate stitch, being linked and interconnected; I felt it represented the way #107days was linking people in the search for justice for Connor. However, replacing the number would have been difficult and risked damaging the background fabric, so I sent it off as it was – not perfect, but done with care, love and a lot of thought.

That seemed about right.

Other patches were explicitly meaningful such as the patch with a small gauze bag containing felt shells, and the numerous double-decker buses. There were many political messages, including quotes from disability activists and the blunter 'We have moved on from 1970, have you?' or simply, 'ENOUGH'. A textile artist from the USA created a reproduction of the American Declaration of Independence.

Just under 300 patches were created out of a wide range of materials and method. This included several patches from a Messy Church group in Kent.

Janet said that when she initially laid the patches out on her living room floor and got a sense of what the quilt might look like, she cried. A few months later, after an enormous amount of work and fiddling about (in true #JusticeforLB form, the request for patches to be a particular size was not always followed and none of the three quilters had made a quilt before), it was finished. A truly breathtaking piece of outsider art.

No matter how many times I look at it, I see something new. The colour, the pictures, the materials are spectacular, and the way in which it is woven together is exceptional.

Measuring around 2.7m by 1.2m, it even has the names of each person who created a patch printed on the back.

The quilt has been exhibited in the Manchester People's History Museum, the Yorkshire Sculpture Park, Lancaster and Newman Universities, the Disability Studies International biannual conference, The King's Fund and in Avilés, northern Spain. Helena Kennedy, QC, arranged for it to be hung in the hallway at Mansfield College, Oxford, where she is the Principal.

You can see full-colour images of the quilt at this link: https://mydaftlife.com/2014/09/04/resistance-stitching-and-the-justice-quilt/

Summer 2015: Verita 2 and the Mazars findings

Rich and I were in Chicago attending the Society for the Study of Social Problems conference with Mark Sherry when we received a copy of Verita 2 in the summer of 2015.[4]

---

4   This was the broader review of Southern Health actions that NHS England had commissioned after the first investigation, which focused only on what happened in the Unit, was published.

I sat in the computer room in the hotel and speed-read the report. Another horrible read. The investigation examined the takeover process of the Oxford provision by Southern Health and found that a series of errors had happened during this process; most importantly, the two key Southern Health people involved in the takeover handed their notice in just before the takeover happened, and Katrina Percy decided on a 'business as usual' approach for the newly acquired provision.

Both of these actions magnified problems, as Oxfordshire staff, expecting a fresh start and new management, were left with little sign of the bright new future they were anticipating and had been promised. The report carefully detailed further errors in senior management but seemed to randomly conclude there was no evidence that these failings contributed to Connor's death. The two 'lay members' of the investigation, George Julian from Team LB and Bill Love who had been selected by NHS England, stepped down from being associated with the review as they could not agree with the conclusions given the evidence detailed.

The report found the following:

The post-acquisition model of 'business as usual' adopted was flawed because significant concerns had been raised about the quality of management in Ridgeway [the Oxfordshire provision]. Southern Health divisional managers needed to fully engage with managers and clinicians in Ridgeway to ensure that the board level executives could rely on the reports they were receiving.

It was combined with little or no contact from the Hampshire-based Trust:

Ann Nursey (a former commissioner at the County Council) wrote to the chief executive of Southern Health on 19 February 2013 complaining about the lack of contact from senior managers at Southern Health. The letter says that since the acquisition 'our experience so far has been very disappointing' and asking who is now managing the learning disability services.

Meanwhile, early findings from the Mazars review were shared with us that same summer. Out of 337 unexpected deaths of learning-disabled people between 2011 and 2015 within Southern Health, only two were investigated, one of which was Connor's. George Julian texted these figures when I was on the bus home from work. I remember staring at the text, tears streaming. The other passengers on the bus faded away as I sat there, in utter horror that things were so much worse than we imagined.

The ease with which so many people had been forgotten without any consideration of how and why they had died was simply incomprehensible. But of course, it wasn't. Connor's death had been badged 'natural causes' from the moment it happened, and, over two years later, at the first pre-inquest review hearing.

1 October 2015: the week before the inquest

A week or so before the start of the inquest, Southern Health were still disclosing records to us they should have provided two years earlier. The contempt with which we were treated remained battering. I went off work 'sick' that week after a lovely GP colleague asked me why I was in our office staring, with a tangled, overwrought and exhausted expression, at the latest communication from the Trust.

John Lish's earlier prediction that the drawbridge was being raised was spot on as Southern Health cut adrift various staff members and, by the start of the inquest, there were seven separate legal teams, each led by a barrister, representing the Trust and six staff members.[5] One brief was appointed only days before the inquest started.

The inquest loomed as something so enormous, something so fucking serious and important and unavoidable, and yet something I would saw my own leg off to avoid. We knew that a determination (verdict) that didn't capture how deeply Connor had been failed would forever haunt us.

---

5   The Trust represented staff where there was no 'conflict' in interest. There was separate representation for staff members with different stances to the Trust.

Your grave is getting a collection of buses on it, matey. It's in the woodland bit which isn't supposed to have stuff in it, but I think the cemetery police look the other way.

The cemetery police, Mum? Are there cemetery police, Mum?

Not real police but people in charge of the cemetery.

Why, Mum?

I dunno. I suppose the grave of an 18-year-old boy with a few buses, trucks and a ring of shells around it ain't a big deal really.

CHAPTER 9

The Inquest

The inquest was scheduled to take place in October 2015, and to last two weeks.

We had a supportive team around us. Rosie and her boyfriend Jack, Tom, my mum, my sister Tracey and George Julian planned to attend it all, together with me and Rich. Will and Owen were both at university, so came for the latter part. My dad, our niece Clare, friends and Rosie's mates planned to dip in and out.

As it was, everyone attended as often as they could: friends, colleagues, Selen from INQUEST, Connor's teachers, supporters who I'd met through Twitter. There was a remarkable atmosphere of collectivity and commitment.

George Julian moved in with us for the duration, sleeping on a campbed in the downstairs back room (the 'Justice shed'). She came equipped with her laptop, phone and tablet, power packs and plugs, and set up a social media station on our row in the courtroom. She tweeted the entire inquest when the jury were sitting. The Coroner agreed to this, as long as the sections that took place without the jury present were not made public, and once he was reassured that tweeting wouldn't interfere with the recording equipment.

This was the first time an inquest was 'live-tweeted' and George demonstrated a remarkable ability to tweet the essence of what was unfolding, stripped of added commentary or emotion.

This was quite a feat given the shite that was soon lobbed around. A new Twitter account, @LBInquest, was set up, the hashtag #LBInquest established, and the story quickly gained followers. To give you an idea of the eclectic bunch of followers we had amassed, they included various charities including Just for Kids Law and the Justice Gap, Daniel Sandford, the BBC Home Affairs Correspondent, Dr Maxwell Mclean, a criminologist, Fiona Ritchie, Managing Director at Learning Disabilities, Turning Point, Emma Protheroe, a student nurse, Dee Speers, mental health campaigner, and various other self advocates, journalists, academics, health and social care professionals and human rights specialists. It was apparent from the retweets and discussion that people were gripped by the unfolding process of the inquest.

A solicitor I recently met said, *'My productivity across those two weeks plummeted.'*

The Coroner's Court

Here is Team LB member John Lish's description of the court, with his characteristic clarity and thoughtfulness, from the guest post I mentioned earlier:

The journey to the Coroner's Court was somewhat metaphorical in nature. While I have visited Oxford a few times in the last few years, this was the first time I had used the Park and Ride scheme provided by Oxfordshire County Council and it was well laid out, efficient and even provided free wifi on the buses. It felt like a warm welcome to Oxford. That feeling changed when I approached New County Hall itself. It was built in the early 70s having been designed…in-house and you can tell that it was. I would say there was a nod to Brutalist architecture, but that would be an insult to the architects involved in that movement. It is a building you don't want to gaze upon. Look at the city it says, don't look at me.

The feeling of discomfort continues with its public entrance, which is hidden from the main street around a corner. It gives a sense that you're entering a different world away from the public discourse. This is a building designed for its internal workings and not for engagement with the public space. The foyer containing the reception feels little more than a corridor. Your eyes search for orientation, you see signage for the Coroner's Court and follow the arrow around the corner. You're presented with a multiple choice of closed doors. To your left are lifts and a stairwell, in front are a set of closed doors to a corridor and on your right another corridor behind closed doors and no obvious signage or flow to the building. You spot that the doors on the right are controlled by a push button, so head on down that corridor.

At the end of the corridor is another set of closed doors. Behind that another corridor that runs left, but you need to head straight on into a room which contains a cafeteria. From the doorway, you see wood panelling running along the far wall. Only with a closer look can you see the doors that lead to the Coroner's Court itself and the notices on the doors are small enough so that users of the cafeteria can be oblivious to whether the Coroner's Court actually exists behind the panelling.

So with help, I was shown into the court itself and said goodbye to the 1970s building to enter what looks like a 19th-century court that had been juxtaposed further to add to the Kafkaesque experience. While I generally approve of maintaining usage of heritage, I suspect the seating in the public gallery was designed to minimise the amount of public scrutiny when it was built, let alone the size and needs of people today. It was just another small piece of alienation (and back pain) to add to the experience.

There is a small yet significant low-level hostility in how New County Hall operates to an outsider. It demands you conform and learn its design rather than be openly readable. It doesn't behave like a public space but rather a private space that grudgingly allows public engagement. Its architectural language does remind me of the criticism Sara has faced, in being told by Oxfordshire County Council's Director of Social Care that 'You do things the wrong way... We offered you a meeting when we sent the report and you put your comments online for other people to read.' In other words, you must conform to their behaviours and collude in their private sphere.

The jury

The inquest began with much rustling, moving around and arch-lever-file balancing by the eight barristers, their solicitors and the Southern Health contingent, which included Medical Director Lesley Stevens, their in-house solicitor, barrister and various other people across the two weeks.

The yellowy-cream wooden-panelled courtroom contained the Coroner's throne-like chair on a platform with his court officer sitting directly below. Along the left-hand side was the press box facing the jury box on the right. A front pit consisted of rows of benches for legal teams with a large table in front of the first row. Behind the front pit were steps down to a tunnel to the prison, and then the staggered benches of the public gallery. Tall windows along the wall behind the jury box offered sight of the sky but nothing else. The space oozed the intensity and gravity of the case.

An A4-framed photo of Connor was placed on the corner of the Coroner's desk, facing the jury and the public gallery. We changed the picture at the end of the first week to make sure the jury remained mindful of the young man who had died such a preventable death.

There had been much consternation around making sure the jury members were not followers of my blog during the pre-inquest meetings, and before the jury were brought into the courtroom for the first time there was a further one hour and 16 minutes of deliberation over this issue on the first morning.

The Coroner re-opened the inquest:

Good morning, we are now going to resume the inquest into the death of Connor Sparrowhawk who died on 4 July 2013.

[Howl.]

After running through the exclusionary factors for jury members, including working for Southern Health or the County Council, or if they knew Connor, or our family, he continued:

> *There are a couple of other things I just want to ask you as well. I also want to inquire whether any of you have followed or follow Dr Ryan's, that is Connor's mother's, social media, blogs, tweets and the like in respect of the JusticeforLB campaign and the LB inquest blog and also any social media also in respect of Southern Health.*
>
> *That's a 'no' from all of you I think, isn't it? Thank you. Good. And you mustn't do that.*

Job done.

A day later, a further jury-related issue emerged when Dr Murphy and her husband arrived at the inquest from Ireland, where she now worked. Before the jury were recalled after lunch, Dr Murphy's barrister told the Coroner that a juror had worked with her husband ten years earlier. This generated lengthy discussion about the best way of finding out if this was the case, if she should be isolated and asked, or asked in front of everyone, how the question should be phrased, and so on and so on and so on. Eventually, the jury were called back in.

> *Thank you members of the jury. If you turn to the jury bundle [arch lever file] you'll see, on page 1, a list of witnesses, only a couple of whom we've seen so far. But these are the witnesses who are coming to give evidence, the ones obviously in red,*

in person. I wonder if you could glance down through that list of people and put your hand up or indicate to me if you think you may know any of those witnesses.

Silence.

Can I ask, I'm sorry to single you out, the lady on the end of the second row. Dr Murphy, could you put your hand up? Do you know whether, do you know Dr Murphy and have you ever worked with her?

Head shake.

No? OK, it may be a case of mistaken identity.

There was a faint absurdity about this claim, and the challenges it seemed to present. I didn't know whether to laugh or cry. Connor would be utterly fascinated and absorbed by this case of 'mistaken identity'.

Mum? Did she know her, Mum? Did Dr Murphy know the juror, Mum?

She said she did.

Why, Mum?

I don't know. I suppose she thought she did.

Mum. Did the jury member know Dr Murphy, Mum?

She said she didn't, no.

Mum, did the juror know Dr Murphy's husband, Mum?

No. Well, she wasn't asked that, to be honest.

Why, Mum?

I don't know…

Back in the day, we would have concocted a juicy sub-plot about Dr Murphy, the juror and her husband. We would have come up with various storylines and threads involving Interpol, the CIA and British intelligence, with the odd break for Connor to recover from the silent and exquisite mirth he would often dissolve into. But those days were gone. We were, instead, poring over process and the detail of his death.

The family room

We had use of a family room for the duration of the inquest – a good-sized room kitted out with large, navy-blue settees and arm-chairs off a corridor behind the courtroom. It was an important space given that public access to the courtroom was through the canteen where the various legal teams, Trust and County Council staff milled around. There was some relief in leaving the intensity of the courtroom by the back door, for somewhere we could breathe deeply, be still and wait for the next battering.

My mum and Agent T brought packed lunches every day, reminiscent of our school lunches, while the kids and their mates frequented the various fast-food haunts within walking distance. Our definition of 'family' was pretty loose and, as well as our kids, my parents, sister, niece, George and other friends, it became the hang-out place for various other people, while the fusion of takeaway food smells became more elaborate, and gross, over the two weeks.

We tried to time our trips to the toilet from this room to avoid various staff members or legal bods, but this was not always successful. One day Dr Jayawant mouthed at me in an exaggerated manner 'Are. You. OK?' when I inadvertently caught her eye. Another time, Dr Murphy and I did a toilet cubicle swap in an intensely awkward moment. Most of the Unit staff attended the full hearing, sitting scattered around the public gallery.

Various #JusticeforLB supporters, including Chris Hatton, Mark Neary, Liz Piercy and John Lish, turned up on different days, offering their support and solidarity, some travelling long distances. My life-raft mates Fran, Becca and Clare sat in the public gallery most days, Fran having to be restrained from shouting at the Coroner when outlandish statements were made about the services provided by the Trust, which her son was still experiencing.

The Oxfordshire self-advocacy group My Life My Choice organised a stream of supporters to be in the courtroom and, as the days passed, more journalists began to pitch up.

Early days

Paul Bowen, with the support of either Caoilfhionn or Charlotte, led the proceedings from start to finish with expertise and an apparently instinctive grasp of what battles were important to fight and what to leave. His command of inquest law, in-depth knowledge of the documentation in the various bundles and interactions with the other barristers and the Coroner were deeply impressive. Caoilfhionn or Charlotte demonstrated speed, skill and expertise in digging through tomes of case law to provide additional evidence. One of the legal team would also record the proceedings in real time.

Looking back, the inquest gave me the impression of revolving around two main arguments as to why there was no wrong-doing on the part of the Trust or some of the staff members: there was no evidence that Connor had seizure activity while in the Unit, and his mother was to blame.

We knew, from the Verita investigation, that culpability lay squarely with the Trust and commissioners, yet here we were, over 18 months later, with some counsels carefully introducing threads of doubt into the narrative. Threads that intimated there was no evidence that Connor had seizure activity while in the Unit and his mother was to blame. Discounting seizure activity somehow removed the responsibility of staff to provide basic care. Introducing a mother who was impossible to engage with further diluted this responsibility.

There were around 18 witnesses, mostly giving evidence in person across the two weeks, including Rich and me. At times, particularly in the first week, it looked like an impossible task to keep the inquest to the allocated two weeks. Each witness was taken through their evidence by the Coroner and then each of the eight legal teams could ask them questions. In practice, this involved returning again and again to various documents, records and my blog post about Connor's seizure. This had now become 'The Mystery of the Bitten Tongue Episode'.

The first day of evidence involved playing the 999 calls Dr Jayawant and a support worker made on the morning of 4 July 2013. I left the courtroom when the calls were played but later read the transcriptions.

Support worker:

> 'We have a boy who [has] lost conscious[ness] in [the] bath. He is not breathing.'

Dr Jayawant:

> 'Hi, we need an ambulance at the STATT Unit, we have a patient called Connor Sparrowhawk and I believe he has had a seizure.'

> 'You are saying he has had a seizure. OK, where are you calling from?'

After being given the name of the hospital and directions, the 999 operator suggested a four-hour response window during the latter exchange. I was taken back to the call I received on the morning of Connor's death.

His key nurse was with him and would ring if there was any change…

On the second day, Keiran Dullaghan, Connor's key nurse referred to in this phone call, caused a stir by refusing to answer the question:

'Did you at any stage carry out an assessment of Connor's physical health needs that assessed his epilepsy and risk around bathing?'

He invoked Rule 22 of the Coroner's (Inquest) Rules 2013, which allows you to refuse to answer a question on the grounds of self-incrimination. This generated considerable discussion around what it meant and how the jury should be informed of what exercising this right meant. A day later, Connor's other key nurse, Winnie Betsva, caused a different stir when, after she was sworn in, asked the Coroner if she could say something to us. She turned to face us and said she was so sorry about what had happened.

It was the first, genuine, heartfelt apology we had received.

The locked door and continued seizure denial

One thing that was never pinned down during the inquest was what actually happened on the morning Connor died. We found out from the documentation and witness statements that Connor woke up and was going to have a bath before going to visit the Oxford Bus Company. According to the documentation his support worker and key nurse checked on him every 15 minutes until 9.15am when he was found unconscious. Where the decision for 15-minute observations came from was never uncovered, as witness after witness was asked and said they didn't know.

They were both in the nurses' office which was across the corridor from the bathroom, a short distance away. The support worker was doing an online Tesco order in between checking on Connor. The mundaneness of this detail fills me with queasiness. Still. Ticking the '3 for 2' box while Connor drowned feet away.

Their statements and witness testimony provided contradictory evidence about who did what and when. The support worker's evidence revealed that the bathroom door was locked. She used a key to open it before she found him.

Until then, we hadn't been told that the bathroom door had been locked.

So, not only was Connor not supervised in the bath, but he was locked in the room. This was presented as allowing Connor the privacy to do 'what boys do in the bathroom'. It was never made clear who locked the door. When it was raised a second time, one or two barristers leapt up to say that we did not know if the door was 'locked' – this in spite of the evidence given by the support worker that she had 'used a key to open it'.

Thinking back to Connor bathing at home in the downstairs bathroom with no door, and a constant in-and-out of talking to him, reminding him to wash his hair, chatting to him and answering his endless questions, I felt physically sick. In 18 years, we had never left him in the bath with the door shut, let alone locked. Big Sue and Tina said that, on residential school trips, they would always stand by the door of the shower and talk to the kids, even those without epilepsy.

Sitting there in full view of the jury and listening to the evidence – 'I checked…oh no, he checked' sort of stuff – my brain was screaming: 'What the actual fuck were you doing?

Who checked? When? Did you ever fucking "check"? Or did you suddenly wonder where he was?' The contradictory evidence over who checked and when was never fully addressed during the inquest.

Dr Murphy and more

Staff evidence exhibited a mix of remorsefulness, defensiveness, reflectiveness and the downright offensive. The hardest to sit through was Dr Murphy, which spread from the Friday afternoon in person to the following Monday by video link from Ireland.

We knew from the Verita review that Dr Murphy had assessed that Connor had not had a seizure on 20 May. She took his subsequent statement that he remembered biting his tongue when angry as the accepted version of what happened without discussion with us. The fact that she interacted with Connor a handful of times across the 107 days was irrelevant.

When asked about if Connor had had a seizure, would it be appropriate to leave him in the bath, she replied, *'If it was a proven seizure, it wouldn't have been appropriate.'* She went on to say, *'My understanding is Connor didn't have a seizure while he was on the ward'* – a point the Coroner dismissed, gently reminding her Connor had a seizure on the day he died.

When questioned about the bleedingly obvious point that you don't rule seizure activity out in a patient with epilepsy, she replied, *'I made a judgement call on that day, with all the information I had and I'm always thinking bigger picture and I think that's normal.'*

Paul Bowen QC, making his polite, missile-like points, continued his questioning, drawing on the testimony of expert witness Professor Crawford, a consultant neurologist and Director of the Special Centre for Epilepsy, York.

> *'Dr Ryan had seen her son have seizures in the past.'*

> *'Yes.'*

> *'And she had seen how he presented after a seizure. And she was the best person to know, having seen him that day whether it was likely or not that he had had a seizure, wasn't she?'*

> *'I suppose so.'*

> *'And indeed, I could put it to you that Professor Crawford draws the conclusion that it probably was as a result of an unobserved seizure that he bit his tongue.'*

> *'Well, with all due respect, Professor Crawford wasn't there.'*

> *'I could say the same, you weren't actually there when he was supposed to have had the seizure.'*

No.

Mother-blame revisited

The inquest was obviously a difficult process, and compounded by what seemed to be a continuing tendency to mother-blame. The staff witness statements produced for Connor's inquest offered further examples of this. This set of statements typically included a section headed 'My Relationship with Dr Ryan' or just 'Dr Ryan'. Such a heading was unnecessary for many reasons, not least that Connor clearly had a large family who (apart from Tom) visited him in the Unit and interacted

with staff. It was also odd given I was called Sara in the Unit –
there was no 'Dr' stuff in those days.

Charlotte sent us these witness statements in September
2015 with an email warning us of the content. It's odd really,
contrasting the actions that help or ease, with those that
make a devastating situation worse. Reading the evidence in
advance of Connor's inquest was devastating. For example,
a student nurse who until that point I thought I had got on
well with stated:

> 'I had seen Dr Ryan shouting at a consultant and I did not want
> to experience that. I was scared of her; she was a bit different.'

When something goes catastrophically wrong, pinning the
blame on 'Mum' or the family rather than trying to establish
openly and transparently what went wrong is one of those
aspects of public sector provision that has consistently
floored us over the past few years. Of course, mother-blame
does, in effect, help to relieve a Trust or County Council
from having to think about the pain and grief bereaved
families experience.

It is also indicative of a wider shortcoming in many health
and social care services – of failing to want to understand the
experiences and views of families, and failing to factor this in
when making decisions or statements.

The County Council was also firing nuclear-type missiles
our way. We received an independent report commissioned
by the Director of Adult Social Care one morning, out of
the blue. The report arrived in my inbox two weeks after it
had been circulated to everyone and their dog. It was almost
farcical, as so much of it was inaccurate. It was also deeply

biased, slipping into a review about me and my actions rather than what happened and why.

Days before Connor's inquest began, Alicia Wood, then CEO of the Housing and Support Alliance (now known as Learning Disability England), had forwarded a copy of a letter to Caoilfhionn Gallagher, the human rights barrister who had earlier offered us pro bono support. The letter was from a less reflective Oxford County Council commissioner who had written to two disability activists excusing the Council's role in commissioning such crap services. As I read it, I could see again subtexts of mother-blame.

She described feeling 'immense sympathy' for me while stating, in the same sentence, that she believed my campaigning had done a lot of damage. 'In hindsight' featured, as it does so commonly when something goes catastrophically wrong. We-could-possibly-have-done-more-but-we-were-so-stretched-type bollocks. The letter ends with a toe-curling paragraph which combines 'immensely sorry' with the comment that bloggers have 'a duty to be honest and accurate':

> My hope is that she can find some kind of peace with this, and that one day, she might be able to move on.

Weary Mother, a regular contributor to my blog, captured what the experience is like for many mothers in the following comment on mydaftlife:

> So many of us have fought so bloody hard for justice for our sons and daughters and have all been treated as brutally as Sara and her family has...just for seeking justice. Many of us battle on, like Sara, now.

My son is an actor with a group composed of people with learning disabilities. With tears running down my face I watched him when they performed a play about the First World War. My son was the only soldier from that village to come home. In his tattered uniform he came slowly down the aisle in church, Last Post playing quietly. He leaned heavily on stick (as he now does from damage done to him in real life), his head bandaged and bloody. At front the widows wait with his wife, who moves towards him in beautiful and moving joy.

In the background, slowly and in time to the gently played Last Post, a row of our dead boys walk in line, eyes bandaged and unseeing, comrades all. Arm stretched out, hand on comrade's shoulder.

I wept. So many, so many...so bloody many.

Harm is done to our boys and our girls and like those widows, we are grateful if they just come home.

When cross-questioned at Connor's inquest, the student nurse changed her position and said she was not scared of me. She said I was a mother trying to do her best for her son.

Remembering when you went through a phase of calling me Muv-aaaar all the time.

Yes, Mum.

It used to drive me potty.

Why, Mum?

I dunno. I wish I could hear it again.

CHAPTER 10

Taking the Stand

An earlier death

By Day 4, the pattern of inquest life was becoming familiar: harrowing days, a pint or two in the pub across the road from the court, bus home, nosh dropped off by a mate, further discussion around the kitchen table and falling into bed, exhausted. Submissions, witness questions or notes were emailed by Paul Bowen overnight to read on the bus to County Hall the following morning.

Around us, people would be getting on with their everyday lives: the dog tied up opposite the primary school Connor was excluded from; Oxford Brookes students talking about nights out and coursework at the bus stop; endlessly bored-looking women and men scrolling through their phones before going to work on autopilot; the odd altercation between passenger and bus driver; primary school kids clutching book bags and *Frozen* lunchboxes (from the film).

Back in the family room waiting for another day to start, Paul and Charlotte came in to tell us that information relating to an earlier death, in the same bath as Connor, had been disclosed to the Coroner: a 57-year-old man called

Clive Granger[1] who died in 2006. Some of the same staff were present when both Connor and Clive Granger died.

Over the two years of disclosures, meetings and witness statements, and in the evidence given during the first three days of the inquest, there had been no mention of Clive Granger.

Paul explained that eight months after Connor died, in March 2014, Dr Murphy remembered hearing about another patient dying in the same bath when she was doing her training. She remembered a report written at the time that raised issues around the steepness of the baths.

Dr Murphy banned baths in the neighbouring John Sharich Unit – the Unit that Connor was in had, by this time, closed. The CQC was not impressed with the act of breaching patients' rights to have a bath when they inspected the Unit and Southern Health instigated an investigation into the bath ban.

I'd never seen the bathrooms at the Unit. That there was yet another piece in the 'Connor should never have drowned' jigsaw was almost too much. Another person had died in the same fucking bath. How could someone die such a random death without it leading to the erasure of any risk of another person doing the same?

The Coroner, also shocked, held an in-camera hearing that morning – an exclusive meeting that involved only barristers. The excluded public milled around the canteen with no idea what was going on and the wider social media audience tweeted their impatience to know what was happening. George had agreed to only tweet on the @LBInquest account when the jury were in court.

---

1   A pseudonym.

Again, you have to ask what on earth a bereaved family does with a shocking development like this. We would not have been allowed into the in-camera hearing. We weren't able to make any sense of this new information in the way that the legal representatives could. We were utterly bereft.

Dr Murphy handed in her notice shortly after repeal of the bath ban in the spring of 2014, relinquished her licence in the UK and went to work in Ireland.

It was her barrister who introduced Clive Granger's death into the inquest. As it was, it barely featured other than rocking us to the core.

The idea that Dr Murphy suddenly remembered Clive Granger's death years later in 2014 is in my view unlikely. Being typically social bods means we often share the sensational, the voyeuristic, the shocking, the unusual, which become a kind of circulating folklore. That Connor and Clive Granger died in the same bath must have generated conversations among those present at the time of each death. How could it not? At least two members of staff, Dr Jayawant and Paul Munday, a senior managerial staff member, were present on both days.

At the close of Connor's inquest, the Coroner said he would be issuing a Prevention of Future Deaths report, and would look further into Clive Granger's death and why this was not disclosed earlier by the Trust. A few months later, he sent us copies of three police witness statements taken from Paul Munday, Dr Jayawant and the student nurse present in the bathroom that day, with a letter saying he was going to close the case:

On the basis of the available evidence, I am satisfied that Mr Granger did not in fact drown in the bath and, consequently, there is no need for me to enquire any further into Mr Granger's death as it was from natural causes.

Now I'm no Coroner, nor a medic, but I can't see how establishing that Clive Granger *didn't* drown means he must have died from natural causes. This strikes me as a bit of a leap. Particularly given he had been undergoing involuntary ECT treatment at the time of his death. This could be interpreted as another example of the brushing over of certain deaths despite the layers of apparent process and safeguarding of 'vulnerable people'.

There were also some substantial inconsistencies in the evidence provided in these statements.

I emailed the Coroner asking how he could accept these contradictory statements and he replied to say that inconsistencies are inevitable after so much time. He said also that Southern Health had informed him that Clive Granger's death was not disclosed because they decided there was no link between his death and Connor's.

This surfaced around the time the Mazars review was published, providing incontrovertible evidence that some people do not count, in life or death.

This could have so easily been Connor, 40 years on. Dying through indifference, denied the fundamental rights of investigation into deaths in the care of the state, with the agreement of both the Coroner and the responsible doctor. Tossed aside, without consideration. Form-ticking, a phone call or two, and the swift wrapping up of loose ends with a grubby little 'could not give a shit' bow that no one would ever see.

Without Charlotte's insistence that Connor's post-mortem should be conducted properly and the advice we received from Caoilfhionn and INQUEST – essential specialist, human rights informed advice – we would never have pushed as far as we did. This is advice and support that too often families do not get.

Giving evidence

Giving evidence at Connor's inquest was a truly terrible experience, but the preventable death of a child renders your 'terrible' irrelevant. Listening to the unimaginable, reading the unsayable, realising with even more clarity how Connor's life was simply snuffed out. How he was failed on a scale that has no measurement.

I was called to give evidence on the Tuesday morning of the second week, entering the box for the second time. Barrister and broadcaster Helena Kennedy QC wrote in her classic book *Eve Was Framed: Women and British Justice*[2] the following:

> *A recurrent theme, heard from prisoners and witnesses alike when talking about their courtroom experiences, is the terror of the witness box, the intimidation of the procedure, made worse by the paraphernalia of the wigs and gowns and a language which obfuscates rather than illuminates.*

She went on to write:

> *For the witness or defendant it means having the focus of attention turning on them in an environment which is comfortable only to a small class of people.*

---

2   Kennedy, H. (2005) *Eve Was Framed: Women and British Justice*. Vintage Press (2nd Edition), p.12.

There were no wigs and gowns, and I wasn't on trial, but the context, the setting, the process and the enormity of the whole thing was overwhelming. I steeled myself to keep calm, answer the questions carefully and not swear. The jury had by this time been carefully fed 'monstrous mother' titbits by barristers during various witness testimonies.

Alan Jenkins QC, counsel for Dr Murphy, was first, and carefully outlined his three areas of focus: 1) Connor could not be left home alone; 2) I could have found out Dr Murphy's phone number to ask her questions about her treatment of Connor; and 3) 'Communication'. I felt his first point to be a gendered pop as he linked my working full time into his argument that there was no one to look after Connor at home. It was incredibly difficult to listen to, and I had an overwhelming urge to vault over the witness box, grab the barrister by the throat and snarl, *'Don't tell me I didn't want my boy home, you fucking bastard.'*

I didn't, and the questions continued.

'Can I ask about one further topic: communication? Can we look at page 315 of the notes please? This is, I think if we go down a little bit please, Charlotte Sweeney's note [Charlotte Sweeney was the occupational therapist at the Unit]. This is 22 May 2013 and Charlotte Sweeney indicates that she made a telephone call to you to discuss the pattern of Connor's seizures. Do you remember the call?'

'Yes.'

'And you gave the response that Connor had tonic-clonic seizures in the past and A&E assessments, and he may also have had absence seizures in the past?'

'I wouldn't have said that.'

'You didn't say that?'

'I would have said he definitely had absence seizures in the past. He had several.'

'Was there any difficulty getting across your understanding?'

The barrister continued by raising my 'lack of rapport' with the occupational therapist and student nurse at the Unit. The subtext being, I assume, that I was so difficult to engage with and that nobody in the Unit knew they should supervise Connor's baths.

He returned to the argument that the student nurse was scared of me and I'd shouted at a consultant, despite the retraction of the 'being scared' statement by the nurse during her evidence a week earlier.

'She said she'd seen you shouting at a consultant, not Dr Murphy.'

'She said she saw me shouting "Where's the assessment and treatment?" which is something I asked Dr Murphy in the CPA [care planning meeting] on 10 June and I asked her it in front of a whole room of people. It's minuted that I asked Dr Murphy – I did not shout – "Where is the assessment and treatment?"'

'OK. So she's wrong?'

'Yes.'

He moved on to my blog and a post in which I'd referred to a 'Dr Crapshite'. This was an account of the afternoon I'd phoned the crisis line after Connor had punched Big Sue at school, when the on-call psychiatrist insisted he couldn't help us because he wasn't Connor's consultant. In the post I wrote:

> *'Blimey, that don't matter. Dr Crapshite only saw him once before discharging him, so no big relationship there.'*

In his quietly spoken manner, the barrister asked:

'Did you think this would facilitate an easy rapport with staff; that you were slagging them off in a public forum?'

I don't know. I made anonymous comments about a member of staff who was an amalgam really. The Unit or staff were not named, and this post, like so many, was an expression of my frustration, anxiety and concern that available services were simply not good enough. 'Dr Crapshite' was synonymous with the whole process and experience.

It generated a low ripple of tittering among the public gallery whenever it was mentioned by Dr Murphy's barrister. He'd earlier asked one of the nurses:

> *'Did you see the part of Dr Ryan's blog where she described a doctor as "Crapshite"?'*

The nurse replied, evenly:

> *'No, not particularly.'*

It unfolded during the evidence given by a Band 6 Nurse that Dr Murphy left a meeting I had attended calling me toxic and some other, undisclosed expletive. From what we could piece together from the evidence given at the inquest, Dr Murphy and the community psychiatrist were deeply offended by my blog post and 'Dr Crapshite'. How much this affected the decisions Dr Murphy made about the 'care' provided to Connor is something which deeply troubles me.

After barrister Alan Jenkins QC sat down, it was the turn of Roderick James QC, who was representing the Unit manager. He focused on one point: me not telling the staff that Connor needed to be observed in the bath.

> 'Please, I preface this by saying I make it absolutely clear this is not a criticism, I just want to make sure about what you say about it… Do you accept that on none of those occasions – Dr Johnson filling out the admission form, and speaking to Charlotte Sweeney in early April – on all occasions that bathing was being raised, do you accept that there was no mention of the need to observe and the fact that you did observe Connor?'

> 'Yes.'

> 'Thank you.'

There. Through a combination of working full time, writing a blog about our experiences of health and social care, failing to tell staff in a specialist unit to observe a young patient with epilepsy in the bath, and calling a consultant 'Dr Crapshite', I killed Connor.

I added that I would no more have asked staff to observe Connor in the bath than ask a school teacher, taking any one of our kids on a school trip, to not let them loose near a motorway. It was a level of care so basic, it didn't cross my mind to raise it after Connor had the seizure in May, or when I spoke to Charlotte that day.

The portrayal of me and so many other women as unbalanced troublemakers (at best) throughout this process demands critical reflection by those directly involved in the mother-blame game, and by those who stand by and witness it happening without comment. Mother-blame is a form of suppression and silencing in the UK. A colleague of mine said that, in Greece, parents would be vilified for not complaining about poor services and support for their children. She could not understand what we were being subjected to.

The second barrister finished his questions and there was a lunchbreak. Under oath and unable to discuss my evidence, I wandered out to the street, dazed. I caught up with life-raft mates Clare and Becca who were on their way to Costa's in the Clarendon Centre. We spent the 40 minutes or so not really talking about anything. Back in the courtroom, I waited to continue my evidence sitting on my own in the pew behind the witness box. I remember the utter sadness I felt. Missing Connor and worrying about how the kids were dealing with sitting through this shite.

Back in the box, the Coroner offered the question baton to the remaining five barristers.

'Mr Williamson?'

'No questions, Sir.'

'Mr Samuel?'

'My client has instructed me to ask no questions, Sir.'

Mr Walsh, Mr Fortune, Ms Patterson? No questions. Thank you.

The jury retire

The inquest kept within the two weeks timetabled. Neurology and epilepsy expert witness Professor Pamela Crawford – who was refreshingly informed, sensitive and sensible and attended daily – gave evidence at the end and said that, while her original report demonstrated serious failings, the evidence she'd heard during the inquest made it clear that things were worse than she could tell from the records.

She said that Connor should have been kept in sight or sound when he was bathing and it was clear he'd had various types of seizure activity while in the Unit. She looked directly at me and Rich when she said this. More tears. Over two years after Connor died, to hear someone say in court what we'd known all along was so important.

Charlotte Haworth Hird, who is not a medic, identified several potential episodes of seizure activity while examining the Unit records. These included Connor getting up in the middle of the night and getting dressed without seemingly being aware of this. Staff had recorded these unusual behaviours but no one made the link to possible seizure activity.

After very careful and detailed summing up by the Coroner, the jury were excused on the Thursday afternoon to consider their determination. We went to the pub across the road and later fell into bed in a kind of liminal state. The process had shifted into a different kind of harsh and uncomfortable space, one characterised by even more anxiety, fear and uncertainty. In our two years of interactions with our legal team, Caoilfhionn, Paul and Charlotte, they had always been brutally open about what a mountain climb we were facing in this process.

The next morning, we got up, got ready in various states of wakefulness and communication, and set off once again to catch the bus to town. 'Real life' was on hold.

I took photos across the two weeks. I wonder how much taking photos during the inquest was an expression of trying to maintain some control in a space which was utterly alien, bewildering and coated with overwhelming grief and loss.

The pictures I took that Friday morning capture the sombre, sad, anxious and agitated mood. There were no lunch runs or smelly takeaways that day. Fran gave out #JusticeforLB laminated bus badges and there was a now-packed public gallery that included Connor's retired headteacher, other campaign followers and the press. We had no idea how long the jury would take to reach a determination.

Late morning, Rich and I went outside for some fresh air. We walked past the flat-screen TV in the reception area that had announced 'The Late Connor Sparrowhawk' inquest for two weeks. We were surprised to see various television vans in the car park.

We were given the nod that the jury had reached their conclusion and court would adjourn at 2pm.

The determination

We had no idea what the determination would be, having spent two weeks sitting feet away from nine members of the public tasked with deciding this. I felt sick and fearful that Connor would be further let down by a process that discounted him as human. There had been so much unruly game-playing, in spite of the stamp of coronial authority over the proceedings, that I couldn't be sure whether or not the Trust would be completely exonerated, and Connor's death ruled to be accidental.

The Coroner came in and we stood and did the 'head bow' movement for the last time. (Something never detailed in any inquest instruction manual, but something we did because those around us did.)

There was a delay in the jury being summoned. Eventually they reappeared and sat down awkwardly. The jury filed in for the last time, walking in between the back of our row of benches among the legal teams and the public gallery, with our family in the front row. Our kids and their friends had scrutinised these nine members of the public carefully across the two-week hearing, trying to gauge whether they were sympathetic or convinced by particular evidence. In these discussions, the kids named jurors by the positions they sat in: 'bottom left', 'top right'...

As they had deduced, the lead juror was 'top left'. He stood and carefully read out the unanimous determination, first establishing that Connor had died at the STATT Unit.[3]

Christ. Connor died at the Unit, not at the John Radcliffe hospital. He was dead before I received Fran's text on the bus that morning of 4 July 2013, asking about the school prom. He died on his own, locked in a bathroom, in the shabby Unit he hated.

The determination continued:

Connor Sparrowhawk died by drowning following an epileptic seizure while in the bath, contributed by neglect.

Connor's death was contributed to by very serious failings, both in terms of systems in place to ensure adequate assessment, care and risk management of epilepsy in patients with learning disability at STATT and in terms of errors and omissions in relation to Connor's care while at STATT.

---

3   This was news to me, as I'd left the courtroom when the pathologist gave evidence and had not opened the post-mortem report the Coroner's assistant had thoughtfully sent us in a sealed white envelope with other documents, a year or so earlier.

Contributory factors include:

A lack of clinical leadership on the Unit.

A lack of adequate training and the provision of guidance for nursing staff in the assessment, care and risk management of epilepsy.

A very serious failing was made in relation to Connor's bathing arrangement.

Other failings included:

The failure to complete an adequate history of Connor's epilepsy and complete an adequate epilepsy risk assessment soon after admission.

Evidence also exists of inadequate communication with Connor's family and between staff regarding Connor's epilepsy care, needs and risks.

Like the expert witness Professor Crawford, the jury called out the crap for what it was and pulled no punches in their determination. Having spent over two years dealing with grotesque attempts to make Connor's death something it wasn't, it was an extraordinary relief to hear sense, while utterly devastating.

A press conference was held in the County Council car park: a row of cameras on tripods and journalists holding out chunky grey furry microphones. Years before, when the kids were young, Connor did a massive, unfettered sneeze during tea which blasted Rosie's pasta over the table. After the commotion this caused, Connor would regularly ball his fist like a microphone, shove it under one of our noses and ask,

'Did I sneeze on you? Did I sneeze on you?' Here we were, 15 or so years later, with a row of 'real' mics under our noses.

Charlotte, surrounded by family, friends and campaigners, read out a statement we'd written the evening before. A large motorbike revved up and down the road drowning out much of what she said.

There was a bit of argy-bargy as one journalist asked us what we thought of the apology Southern Health had given us (we hadn't received an apology).[4]

We walked around the corner to a tapas restaurant where we took over the first-floor mezzanine for a sponta-neous 'celebration'. There were around 30 of us, a lovely mix of people: My Life My Choice members, our legal team, family and friends. We ate tapas, drank jugs of sangria, beer and wine, chatted, and engaged in copious selfie-taking –

---

4   Southern Health did an extraordinary number in apologising to us via the press over the years. A resounding failure to understand the apology is about being sorry, not about reputation repair.

enjoying a moment before the legal team would part to head back to their separate lives.

The afternoon drifted into early evening, and as the various news programmes began we set up an iPad on the table and crowded around. In the candlelit space, we watched the news coverage. BBC Oxford included a piece by the brilliantly committed BBC journalist and producer Serena Martin. Serena had interviewed Rosie, Will, Owen and Tom in the family room, talking about Connor a day or so earlier. It was lovely and captured the intense love they felt for their brother Connor, and for each other.

PART V

JUSTICE

CHAPTER 11

Stumbling into Scandal

The Mazars findings

On 10 December 2015, two months after the inquest, Jeremy Hunt, Secretary of State for Health, was called to answer an Urgent Question in the House of Commons. The BBC published a leaked version of the Mazars review earlier that morning. This had the aim of identifying the level of investigation into the expected deaths of learning-disabled people and people with mental-ill health in the care of Southern Health.

Following the endless delay around publishing this review, someone had made the decision to share it with BBC Social Affairs Correspondent Michael Buchanan. The report opened with an acknowledgement which never fails to make my eyes leak. A rare drop of humanity in what typically passes for learning disability 'care':

This report presents a lot of numbers. The team recognise that each number represents a loved one and would like to give their condolences to the families of every person referred to in the following chapters.

The content was harrowing. Just a few extracts to give some idea:

> *There was a lack of leadership, focus and sufficient time spent in the Trust on carefully reporting and investigating unexpected deaths of Mental Health and Learning Disability service users.*

> *30% of all deaths (those reported as expected and unexpected) in Adult Mental Health services were investigated as a CIR (Critical Incident Review) or SIRI[1] (Serious Incident Requiring Investigation), less than 1% of deaths in Learning Disability services were investigated as a CIR or SIRI and 0.3% of all deaths of Older People in Mental Health services were investigated as a SIRI.*

> *Timeliness of investigations is a major concern – on average it took nearly 10 months from an incident to 'closing' a SIRI relating to deaths.*

> *The Trust could not demonstrate a comprehensive, systematic approach to learning from deaths as evidenced by action plans, board review and follow up, high quality thematic reviews and resultant service change.*

> *The average age of death of the 337 service users who died with a Learning Disability was 56. The median age was 59. Further investigation must be undertaken to review the comparability of this finding with that of the CIPOLD inquiry. The involvement of families and carers has been limited – 64% of investigations did not involve the family.*

---

1   SIRIs have to be reported externally and closed by the relevant commissioner.

Jeremy Hunt said:

> *The whole House will be profoundly shocked by this morning's allegations of a failure by Southern Health NHS Foundation Trust to investigate over 1000 unexpected deaths. Following the tragic death of 18-year-old Connor Sparrowhawk at Southern's Short-Term Assessment and Treatment Unit in Oxfordshire in July 2013, NHS England commissioned a report from audit providers Mazars on unexpected deaths between April 2011 and March 2015.*
>
> *The draft report, submitted to NHS England in September, found a lack of leadership, focus and sufficient time spent in the Trust on carefully reporting and investigating unexpected deaths of mental health and learning disability service users. Of 1454 deaths reported, only 272 were investigated as critical incidents, and only 195 of those were reported as serious incidents requiring investigation. The report found that there had been no effective, systematic management and oversight of the reporting of deaths and the investigations that follow.*

Michael Buchanan, a journalist drenched in grit, decency and determination, had a considerable scoop that morning. The coverage was extensive.

Evidence that so many people could die unexpectedly within a single Trust without investigation raised questions, anger and awkwardness, not only for Southern Health but also the CQC, NHS England, NHS Improvement and the Secretary of State. The debate in the Commons that morning, and the House of Lords later that day, demonstrated unusual and appropriate cross-party condemnation and horror.

Hunt asked the health and social care inspectorate, the Care Quality Commission (CQC), to conduct a broader review of investigations into deaths across the NHS and to focus a forthcoming re-inspection of Southern Health on death reporting. The CQC had conducted a full hospital inspection of Southern Health in 2015 and given them a rating of 'Improvement Needed'. Given how bullish the Trust were in insisting that improvements had been made to their death reporting after early indications from the Mazars team about the content of the review, it was shocking that this CQC re-inspection was to find continued failings, early in 2016. The CEO of Southern Health Trust, Katrina Percy, was again in the media spotlight because of the report findings; her ability to hold onto her role was extraordinary. In addition to the #JusticeforLB campaign, there was a growing and strong movement of families and Trust governors, and ex-governors, based in Hampshire, who also kept pressure on Southern Health, attending board meetings and raising concerns.

LB's story spreads

Going back to July 2013, Connor's death was not deemed worthy of 'news' coverage. There was a very slow burn on the interest in what happened to him, and Charlotte Haworth Hird spoke on our behalf for the first requests for interview that dribbled through. My only media experience was several years earlier when I was on a BBC Oxford Radio programme one afternoon to talk about my autism research. After being introduced as an expert in autism – a ridiculously giant leap – I forgot the third of three typically held characteristics of autism. I recognised, with some humiliation but little disappointment, that media appearances were not my bag.

However, as interest grew in what happened, it became clear we would have to step up. It was fortuitous that the first interviews I did were orchestrated by local BBC journalist and producer, Serena Martin. Her focus on holding Southern Health to account, and familiarity with the detail, made the experience easier. She was also very good at saving additional requests until the last minute, when I was already ensconced in the basement of the BBC Oxford studios in Summertown.

'Oh, when you have finished doing the pre-record for drive time, Huw Edwards/the Today programme/South Today are keen for you to be on, it will only take another five minutes...'

Within a short space of time, I got through potentially excruciating and terrifying experiences. Unfortunately, there was a real appetite for 'Mum' all the time, and Rich, who had media experience through his work, and was good at it, was too often either a reserve choice or cut out of the final version (ironically experiencing the 'flip side' of mother-blame).

We went to Salford to appear on *BBC Breakfast* a few times, travelling the night before, falling out of bed after sleep punctuated by eruptions of fear-generated insomnia and walking across a quad to the BBC building, for a 5.45am start. Transformed by serious slap, we would wait to be sneaked into the studio to perch on the bright red settee while a video clip was played. A few terrifying minutes later, another video clip and removal from the studio to catch the train home.

I'd think about Connor on the journey back to Oxford and try to imagine the households across the UK that his beautiful face had been beamed into, and people who might be thinking about him as they started their day. I have no idea what, if anything, people did think about, but I was glad he was rocking national news.

People have asked if I find it upsetting to see Connor's photo on the news so regularly. I'm chuffed to bits that it's become unremarkable rather than extraordinary. The initial disregard with which his death was treated was additionally distressing. That his death, and what it led to, has been the lead story on BBC and other news channels is a positive development.

Connor and #JusticeforLB campaigners have collectively broken through a steadfast barrier to recognise humanity, love, care and brilliance. Danny Tozer, Edward Hartley, Thomas Rawnsley, Richard Handley, Nico Reed, Connor and other young people who died so young are, finally, gaining what should be obvious recognition that what happened to them was wrong and barbaric. Of course, it was the two non-learning-disability-related stories (the mystery caller and contract regularities around Southern Health board execs) that were the biggest headlines in terms of news stations covering the story. Even so, it was a phenomenal achievement to get so much coverage, and testament to the rigour, determination, passion and integrity of various journalists, including Michael Buchanan, Sophie Woodcock, Simon Hattenstone, Serena Martin, Katie Razzall, Hannah Somerville, Jayne McCubbin, Victoria Macdonald, Saba Salman, Andy McNicoll, Chiade O'Shea, Catherine Jones, Clare Sambrook and Katie Goodman, who pushed the typically un-newsworthy into the headlines.

A voicemail message

In April 2016, after one of the many media appearances at that time (this time around the publication of another negative CQC inspection of Southern Health), I went back to work to find an anonymous voicemail from a Southern Health staff member. The message started off innocuously, before a breathtaking swerve:

> *Good morning, hello, hi, this is a message for Dr Sara Ryan, um I've been seeing on the media about your son, your poor son who died in the care of Southern Health. I work for Southern Health and I feel awful that you lost him. I'm so sorry that you have done, it's tragic, and I hope you find some closure after the report, the issue of the GM...er, CQC report today, but I do think you are being very vindictive. I think you are a vindictive cow.*

> *On TV all the time slating the NHS Southern Health. With your intelligent background, you know, as much as much as anyone else knows, that Southern Health only took over those units in Oxfordshire recent, you know the recent months before your son died.*

> *You know, with your background, it takes a while to make changes in anywhere, and I think now you've just become a*

witch hunt and you want some attention, but you are vindictive and you are unpleasant, and you are a nasty cow.

Mother-blame.

I saved the message and, after a brief discussion with Rich and George, we published the message on the #JusticeforLB blog. It fleetingly became a big story in moments. The phone didn't stop ringing and we even had Sky News trying to get us in the studio.

The police investigated the call and, after a bit of digging, the name of the staff member was passed to them. She said she was sorry. It was a heat of the moment type thing.

The extraordinary board meeting

On 10 January 2016, Southern Health held an extraordinary board meeting to discuss the Mazars review. It was attended by various members of Team LB, our family and other families affected, or potentially affected, by the Trust's failings.

The meeting was a shambles from the start. The Trust underestimated the size of the public audience, and the executive board ended up sitting comfortably round a horse-shoe-shaped table, while the rest of us were squashed at the back of the room, many standing, for the three-hour meeting. Both ITV and BBC News filmed the meeting.

The mood in the room was tense from the outset and there were regular interjections from the audience. Each answer or non-answer from the increasingly uncomfortable-looking board members raised further anger.

Tom had said he wanted to ask Katrina Percy a question the weekend before the meeting but didn't say what. At the end of the meeting, nearly three hours later, there was a dedicated spot for public questions, but I was surprised when he put his hand up.

> *'I thought it was extremely inappropriate that you'd even say that you might have added to our grief as a family, when you definitely piled it on.'*

Katrina Percy apologised. Tom continued:

> *'This is the first time I've heard an apology and I've had to ask for it, and I'm 16 and this is a room full of adults, you know, it's not easy and I didn't want to do it. I've had to do it because you guys haven't apologised.'*

You could have heard a pin drop really. Tom brought into the meeting the human cost: the brothers and sister who not only lost a brother but also had to deal with an enormous battle and the accompanying rage, despair and the duress we were constantly and needlessly under. He fired a well-aimed arrow at a bunch of ineffective executive board members who had 'led' a consistently failing organisation for four years with little or no apparent hint of remorse, concern or recognition that a growing number of bereaved families, and other members of the public, had had enough.

Another question was posed by my 'life-raft' mate Becca to the CEO and Board Chair:

'We are clearly in the wrong place. Can you tell us who we should be talking to? Who is your boss?'

A member of the public, Sarah Snow, said:

'For a parent of a young person with autism and learning disabilities, the Mazars report reads like an apocalyptic nightmare. Throughout this process, individuals and families have been treated with institutional, and sometimes personal, contempt... You have in fact now created a situation where the services that people may need are no longer accessible because individuals and families do not have confidence in the quality of the services provided and are therefore choosing not to use them. This cannot be tolerated.'

And from Shaun Picken, from My Life My Choice:

'Katrina, you were clearly struggling. Why didn't you ask for help?'

There were no sensible or coherent answers from the board and the meeting ended with the mood as tense as it had begun. Tom and I hitched a ride home with the My Life My Choice crew, a refreshing journey after the intensity of the meeting.

Coverage of the meeting was due to be on the 6pm news, but David Bowie's death dominated the news. Later that evening, BBC journalist Michael Buchanan texted to say coverage of the meeting would be on the 10 o'clock news. Surprised, we watched the programme in awe that Connor's picture would appear on the same programme as David Bowie. Another of his idols.

Tom by this point had begun to feel nervous about the possibility of appearing on the news. A young man articulately holding an executive board to task would be an obvious clip to pick out in any coverage and I began to worry, but within seconds of his appearance his phone started pinging with 'well done' messages.

It was an extraordinary day, not least because of the death of the writer of *All the Young Dudes*.

I often think about that last holiday we had as a family. In Herefordshire with that shouty sheep we called Rapid Dave. Do you remember?

Yes, Mum.

You kids got the meat sweats after the Sunday lunchtime carvery in the local pub.

Yes, Mum. Was it the meat sweats, Mum?

Yes. Gawd, we laughed and groaned walking back up that hill afterwards.

Did we go on the bus, Mum?

Yep. We caught the bus to Kington one day. I can't remember the number but it was a tiny little bus…

461, Mum. Sargeants' Buses, number 461, Mum.

You know I think about you all the time, don't you matey?

Yes, Mum.

CHAPTER 12

Crime and Justice

In parallel to the inquest and inquiries ordered by health and social care organisations, we had been in touch with the police from the outset. We first met Detective Constable Charlie Ellis of the Thames Valley Police in the relatives room at the hospital on the morning Connor died.

He came in with a colleague to talk to us about what had happened. They were sensitive and reassuring sitting side-by-side in the small space. At the same time, it was as if we were watching a film, or an episode of *Casualty* in which a child's death was kind of glaringly wrong, but at the same time being presented as understandable. They said something like 'it looked like there were no suspicious circumstances'.

While in a state of shock, we managed to drum up enough energy to refute this and assert that Connor should not be dead. I wonder with hindsight if the 'natural cause' discourse was already circulating among the Unit staff. It was, given the experience of Clive Granger and countless, unknown others, one they were familiar with.

I don't think DC Ellis, who we came to know as Charlie, could have imagined on that morning in 2013 that he would be involved in a subsequent investigation into Connor's death for almost four years.

By the time we wrote The Connor Manifesto for our meeting with David Nicholson almost a year later in March 2014, we firmly believed there should be a corporate manslaughter charge brought against the Trust. The police had carefully gathered and examined evidence to see if the bar for prosecution had been reached. We had several meetings with Charlie, one of which was in the Thames Valley Police Commissioner's office. I remember sitting in awe at the police memorabilia around the room: photos, old police hats and helmets. Connor would have bloody loved it.

I'd taken him to an open day at Oxford Magistrates Court when he was about 12. It coincided with a time at school when the focus was on learning how to ask questions. A 'court case' was re-enacted involving a 14-year-old boy who had been caught driving a stolen car. Connor's arm pinged up with question after question, including: 'Would he lose his driving licence?' The magistrate answered each question with thoughtfulness and care.

Much later, after I had received the anonymous voicemail in April 2016, it was Charlie who visited us to update us after he had met with the caller. Rich, struggling to contain his anger and upset at how much sensitivity was being shown to them given what we continued to endure, went for a walk. Tom pitched up before Charlie left and asked if he could ask some questions about police work. After going through 'Do you watch *Luther*?' type questions, he asked Charlie, hypothetically, if one of our family had done what Southern Health had done, like provide poor care, obstruct, prevaricate, lie and fail to disclose various documents or previous deaths, after someone died in that care, would we face charges? Charlie, answering these questions with similar consideration and respect as the magistrate, said yes, quite possibly.

In February 2017 he came around again, this time with his sergeant to tell us that they had sought informal advice from the Crown Prosecution Service who had advised that the evidence was not enough to meet the 'gross negligence' bar. The case was to be closed.

Alongside this police investigation a Health and Safety Executive (HSE) investigation had been set up after Norman Lamb's intervention in 2015. Health and safety law is different from criminal law and Charlie told us that there was a better chance of conviction via the HSE route. By January 2017, the HSE had appointed a barrister specialising in health and safety law to examine whether there was a case to answer. On 9 May 2017, it confirmed that it would prosecute the Trust over Connor's drowning, to which Norman Lamb responded, 'better late than never'.

What I've learned through this process is that investigators – whether the police, HSE or other regulatory bodies – need to be timely in their actions, keep families as informed as they want to be, and try to imagine what it must feel like to be in these situations.

Humanity and basic decency are so important in easing the extraordinary pain experienced, and both Charlie, and latterly Chris Taylor, the Principal Inspector from the HSE, knew this, getting in touch regularly even if there was nothing to update. Both were also good at setting expectations, which is also important.

In reality, families are typically kept in a 'limbo' state, with investigations dragging on for years.

Simple stuff, but it makes a difference to feel that effective investigations are both being conducted and that you matter enough to be updated about them. Having to ask continually if there are any developments makes you feel as if you are pissing in the wind on a deserted and freezing mountain top.

Jeremy Hunt

By 2016, Southern Health had lost the contract to provide services in Oxfordshire, and the STATT Unit, Slade House, was left almost empty. In the original takeover of the site by Southern Health, the Oxfordshire commissioners had failed to include a clause to prevent Southern Health 'keeping' the site, worth a fortune, in the event of failing to deliver what they had promised. This led to a substantial fight to prevent

Southern Health from selling it and walking off with the profit – a fight in which we were more than prepared to chain ourselves to the railings.

Early in 2016, Rich and I, our local MP Andrew Smith, who became a key campaigner to stop the sale of Slade House, and Deb Coles CEO of INQUEST met with Jeremy Hunt to talk about the Slade House site and the issue of the poor care and treatment of learning-disabled people. The one-hour meeting was reduced to 30 minutes because he was delayed and it was clear from pretty much the opening moments that he wasn't going to listen to us.

Deb and I met before the meeting and had a chuckle working out how to airdrop a photo between our phones. The only highlight of the meeting for me was when Deb, with her new-found technical knowledge, clocked that Jeremy Hunt was also wearing a Fitbit and had a mild panic that her Fitbit might start talking to the Fitbit of the Secretary of State for Health. I wondered if it might have resulted in a more productive discussion.

With an enormous amount of behind the scenes manoeuvring, we received confirmation in Spring 2017 that Oxford Health, which were to take over providing services in Oxfordshire, would keep the Slade House site.

Introducing the mermaids

Connor became interested in mermaids, after watching *The Pirates of the Caribbean* one weekend, when he was 16. In his characteristic way, he began to talk about mermaids and ask many questions about them. Big Sue took this new interest seriously and, one Monday afternoon, drove him to Marston in the school minibus to throw a message in a bottle into the river. I later asked him what he'd written to the mermaids:

'Dear Mermaids, do you exist or don't you? From Connor.'

A few weeks later he received a letter and a red net pouch with shells in it. The mermaids confirmed they did exist and told him to sleep with the shells under his pillow to help him dream of them. His adventure with the mermaids was to continue for the next year or so, as he received postcards from them from various sunny spots across the world, coinciding with various teachers' holidays.

He enjoyed his mermaid interlude, which was replaced by the television comedy, *The Inbetweeners*. This coincided with a placement his teacher organised for him at an organisation called TRAX, which did mechanics training for 'disadvantaged' young people just on the edge of the ring road. Connor wore a set of overalls and worked on a Nissan car engine all morning with other activities in the afternoon.

He thoroughly enjoyed this work but was initially outraged at the students smoking during breaks. Big Sue, who went with him, had to do some repair work to ease the tension this caused. Within weeks, Connor sat in the smoking area too, vigorously puffing away on an imaginary fag.

Late 2016, the #JusticeforLB campaign, Charlotte and INQUEST were nominated for a Liberty Human Rights 'Close to Home' award. Rich and the kids attended the ceremony in London. The award, which we won, was presented by the lead actor, Simon Bird, from *The Inbetweeners*. Another one of those Rodgers Coaches moments. I don't think I would have been surprised if a mermaid had pitched up to present it alongside him.

Rolling heads

A few months after the extraordinary board meeting, the replacement of Southern Health Board Chair Mike Petter with Tim Smart was announced in May. Tim was a troubleshooter who was the ex-CEO of King's College NHS Foundation Trust, among other NHS roles, and was selected by NHS Improvement – the organisation responsible for overseeing foundation trusts and NHS trusts. This was a big deal. From where we were sitting, any 'action' was something.

As it turned out, I don't think this was a sensible appointment. In June 2016 Tim Smart attended a meeting in Oxford with My Life My Choice in which he told us that he had offered his services to NHS Improvement after watching Tom's questions in the extraordinary board meeting on BBC News in January 2016. Whether or not this was true, I do know, sitting in that room, that it was a heart-sink moment when he said he had not read the Mazars review because 'it was wrong'.

He headed back to Southern Health HQ where he was tasked by NHS Improvement to investigate whether the executive board members were fit for purpose. Four weeks later, he announced he'd found 'no evidence of negligence or incompetence of any individual board member'.[1]

Michael Buchanan's careful and meticulous journalistic focus for the BBC was to again pay off in July 2016 when he broke a story about Southern Health and contract irregularities. It turned out that a company called Talent Works had received more than £5m from the Trust, after

---

1   In March 2017, the replacement, interim Chair, Alan Dawes, announced that all non-executive directors would be standing down.

winning a contract valued at less than £300k a few years earlier to provide training. Talent Works CEO Chris Martin and Southern Health Trust CEO Katrina Percy were 'former acquaintances' according to the BBC.[2]

This news was astonishing, particularly in light of the compulsory training given to middle management and above that some staff members commented on:

I went on Going Viral while at Southern Health. It was compulsory regardless of how busy you were. Insistent on overnight stay in the hotel even though I lived 20 mins away. It was awful. Crap management twaddle. Every session we had to 'check in', no thought for people like me who were not comfortable sharing in public. I gained nothing from the whole hideous experience.

Yes I'm embarrassed to admit that I'm a Southern Health employee [...] Some of us have been on Going Viral and Gone Viral (there really is no opt-out for certain pay bands) and while of course finding some of it interesting and sort of useful (especially meeting clinical staff and even patient advocates and hearing about their challenges), have come away feeling it's too much corporate nonsense, with ice-breaking tasks and dreaded role-play scenarios.

Within days, Talent Works announced it was withdrawing from the remaining contract work with Southern Health.

The pressure continued into August 2016 when the *Daily Mail* ran a story with the snappy headline '*Eye-popping pensions of shamed NHS bosses at an under-fire mental health trust slammed over patient deaths*'. The story featured large

---

2   www.bbc.co.uk/news/uk-england-36922039

colour pictures of Southern Health Chief Executive Katrina Percy alongside Medical Director Dr Lesley Stevens and Chief Operating Officer Dr Chris Gordon with their salaries stamped over them.

By September, after our incredulity had been stretched to an unimaginable point, Tim Smart announced that Percy was stepping down from being CEO but was to move to a new role for which she was 'uniquely qualified' on the same salary. He later admitted that no due processes had been followed in making this shift[3] and it was later established that Percy had been doing the work involved in her new job as 'part of her portfolio as CEO' since March 2015.[4] My fingers are actually tingling typing these details. This is a public sector organisation, using public money, in full public view, behaving in ways that trounce the seven principles of public life which anyone who works as a public office-holder are expected to follow: selflessness, integrity, objectivity, accountability, openness, honesty and leadership.

You can imagine the response to this latest development. The story of a Chief Exec of an NHS Trust documented as consistently failing being 'kid-gloved' into a made-up non-job on a CEO salary was the equivalent of sticking up two fingers at the British public. It's also important to remember the context of austerity and an overstretched NHS in which these events took place.

While Rich, I and others repeatedly asked 'Eh, what? How can this possibly be?', all we could do was continue to blog and tweet and generally try to keep the pressure on in whatever way we could. It's important to reiterate here

---

3   This admission was made during a BBC documentary about the Trust called *Broken Trust* shown on 7 September 2016.

4   www.bbc.co.uk/news/uk-england-37308857

that, over the previous three years, #JusticeforLB campaign stalwarts had maintained a steady and consistent focus in their particular areas of understanding or expertise. These stalwarts included George, the National Forum for Learning Disabled People (and carers), disability studies academics, Liz Piercy, Agent T, Chris Hatton, Mark Neary, My Life My Choice, Learning Disability England and so many others.

Tim Smart resigned on 19 September 2016 citing 'personal reasons'. In early October I was in Berlin for a weekend break with a couple of friends. My phone started ringing with calls from unknown numbers while we were sitting in a stylish cafe drinking coffee. I guessed that something related to Connor was kicking off at home, as my phone rarely rings.

I answered the next call – the *Daily Mail*: Katrina Percy had resigned with a year's salary. She was not allowed to work in the NHS for a further year. Any comment?

What was there to say?

We wandered off to visit the Berlin Wall and East Side Gallery.

#JusticeforLB fights on

As a backdrop to these events, throughout 2016 there had been a kind of macabre dance between Southern Health, #JusticeforLB and the various regulatory bodies.

Team LB was a random and disparate bunch of committed activists who had no hesitation in calling out the crap we continued to see, with an unusual colour, spark and magic. Between the big stories relating to Southern Health, there was some recognition of our wider campaign – one example was being named in the *Health Service Journal*'s 2016 list of the 100 most influential people in the NHS. Connor and the campaign were increasingly known about in the worlds of health and social care.

There were two performances in Connor's memory that year. Jazz singer and health and social care consultant Edana Minghella wrote a short play which was performed as part of a show called *12 Angry Women* at the Brighton Dome in March. She sent me the script and a recording of the song she'd written. It was one of those skin-prickling moments, listening to the song and reading the script.

Edana had brilliantly woven together the essence of blog post extracts with sections pulled from Connor's inquest, creating a compelling ten-minute performance that captured Connor's quirkiness and the harrowing event of his death and aftermath.

A brief extract of the script:

Mother: End of year assembly. A time of celebrating and sobbing. All the kids singing their hearts out: voices, shouts, words, signs. Everyone rummaging around for tissues within seconds. Right here, right now, our kids have no limits.

(beat)

Generic Official Person (GOP): (addressing someone off stage) It's your evidence that...?

Mother: I'm winded...

GOP: It's your evidence that Connor should not...?

Mother: Winded by...

GOP: It's your evidence that Connor should not have been left for 15 minutes in the bath...?

Mother: Indescribable...

GOP: It's your evidence that Connor should not have been left for 15 minutes in the bath with the door locked?

Mother: Indescribable loss.

Our family headed to Brighton and stayed in a hotel on the seafront. The play had a cast of three (a Generic Official Person, Boy and Mother), and after just a few minutes into the play, the packed audience, who had been having a good old belly laugh, were rendered completely still. Actress Leann O'Kasi sang the song exquisitely.

A Mother's Song – Blues in A Minor, Edana Minghella
I see you laughing at the bus stop
I see you laughing in the dentist's chair
I see you laughing on the floor with the dog
But the first time I saw you you were crying
My bundle of joy
My laughing boy

I hear you shouting at the telephone
I hear you shouting at the radio
I hear you shouting at the boy in that room you shared
But the first time I heard you you were crying
My bundle of joy
My laughing boy

(Chorus)
They didn't see you
They didn't hear you
They didn't listen
They didn't know you
My bundle of joy
My laughing boy

I listen hard to all your questions (mostly)
I listen hard to your mum mum mum mum
I listen hard to your stories and your funnies
But the first time I listened you were crying
My bundle of joy
My laughing boy

I know your quirky funny laughing
I know your hopes and dreams, the things that you love
I know your smell and taste and how your skin feels
But when I first got to know you you were crying
My bundle of joy
My laughing boy

Janet Read, Emeritus Professor at the University of Warwick, organised a memorial performance of Tippett's moving spirituals from *A Child of Our Time* at the Warwick Arts Centre on a stormy Sunday afternoon in June – a free performance open to all. Tippett was inspired to compose the piece by the horror he felt at the persecution of Jewish people by the Nazis; he also wanted the music to carry a universal message about the suffering of all who face oppression. The choir sang on the ground floor of the Arts Centre with the #JusticeforLB quilt behind them, while the audience trailed up the circular staircase and onto the first floor. It was a family outing again for us, with my mum joining in the choir – a piercingly beautiful performance.

#CaminoLB

The campaign also spread beyond the UK in 2016. The idea of holding a #JusticeforLB exhibition in Spain was hatched by Alicia Wood. Alicia, a #JusticeforLB stalwart, was, by this time, heavily involved in a new organisation called Learning Disability England. Alicia, her partner Henry Iles and Mariana Ortiz, who works with Alicia, have strong connections with a town called Avilés in northern Spain and they were keen to spread the story of what happened to Europe.

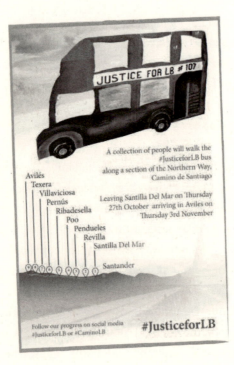

To give it its full name, the Camino de Santiago (sometimes known as the Way of St James) is the name of a series of pilgrimage routes to a shrine in Galicia in north-western Spain. Many follow its routes as a form of spiritual path.

George suggested that we walk the route with a bus made out of cardboard boxes, originally created by a family for the #107daysofaction campaign, all the way from Santander to the proposed exhibition centre in Avilés in time for the International Day of Disability and the exhibition's opening in late 2016.

My dad, a retired draughtsman, made a tarpaulin cover and designed a hinge-type system so it could be folded into three and carried under someone's arm.

We shared details of the proposed ad-venture and people started to volunteer to join us for sections of the journey. My sister, Agent T, was first. She later said she booked the maximum time she could, just under a week, because she thought we'd be walking alone.

Then comedians and good friends John Williams and Dave Griffiths (also known as King Cnut) signed up for the first three days, including the dreaded ferry crossing. Alicia, Henry and Mariana pledged to walk, as did Mariana's daughter. Dawn Wiltshire, Paul Scarrott and Shaun Picken from My Life My Choice[5] were to join us for the last three days with two support workers. Rosie Tozer, whose son Danny had died in a Mencap home the year before after an unsupported seizure, was to join at the same point. Ruth Glynne-Owen, who runs a small autism charity called Blue Sky, signed up for the final 24 hours.

The loosely organised trek was greatly facilitated by Alicia, Henry and Mariana, who dedicated themselves to airport runs and bag drop-offs along the route. I will never forget the moment George, John, Dave and I got off the ferry at Santander after a hilarious and smooth 24-hour crossing involving a pre-Camino celebratory drink or ten, and saw Alicia bouncing up and down, holding a #CaminoLB sign. We had no idea what to expect on this adventure, but Alicia's enthusiasm and passion went a long way to both fuelling and supporting the first few days of the walk.

The Camino is marked by yellow scalloped shells indicating the route, embedded in posts, walls and the pavements of towns. Pilgrim hostels are scattered along the way with an assortment of dormitories and room configurations. The hostels ranged from the cavernous, museum-like building with large double bedrooms that we

---

5   We crowdsourced £2000 to cover the expenses, including passports and walking stuff, for three people from My Life My Choice to join the walk for three days, with two support workers. It was the first time two of them had travelled outside the UK and they came back with firm travel plans for the future. It was as it should be, and obviously can be, but so rarely is.

stayed in on the first night, to a downstairs basement in a village house owned by a woman who gave us brightly coloured, crocheted Camino butterflies after a breakfast of coffee, cake and toast.

We'd set off while it was still dark, walk through woods, along dual carriageways, coastal paths, through cities, towns and villages, along railway lines, fields, tracks and stretches of river and beaches. The sun shone almost the entire time with occasional atmospheric patches of thick mist.

George and I were pretty good at training before the walk began, but neither of us had the time to practise walking the daily 30km we'd set ourselves for the first part of the walk. As it turned out, we managed to do it straightforwardly, with some flagging as it began to cool down and get dark. John and Dave had not trained (sorry guys) but remained good humoured and more than delivered on the comedy front.

The middle days, once John and Dave headed back to the UK, were a mix of George, Agent T and me, joined by Clara, Mariana, Alicia and Henry. On the Sunday afternoon, we walked along the coast and into woodland through a thick mist, choosing to keep walking when we saw a restaurant around midday. After a couple of hours, we were told by someone watching from the balcony of their house by the path that there were no restaurants or cafes open until Ribadesella. We had a makeshift picnic of foraged apples and hazelnuts, and pooled our loot of fruit pastilles, biscuits and dried fruit using the bus as a table.

We posted our progress across the Camino with photos and video footage on Twitter and Facebook. With the sunshine and beautiful scenery, and varying composition of the walking group, the photos were spectacular. It was a soothing and peaceful experience walking miles with the bus clamped to my side, thinking about Connor. Part of the collectivity, simplicity and joy was the passing of the bus from walker to walker as fingers began to numb or arms to ache. This task-sharing demonstrated a thoughtfulness and care contrasting starkly with the 'care' Connor and so many others experienced.

By the time the My Life My Choice crew joined us, with Rosie and Ruth, there was a carnivalesque atmosphere. We walked 15km cheerfully, after a delicious lunch with Asturian cider, and a Spanish TV crew caught up with us as we walked up a hill to the hostel; they interviewed us for local news.

Over the next two days, we were invited to meet local dignitaries and disabled people's groups at the town halls in Gijon and Avilés. Two young school boys waited outside Gijon town hall to hand us a cardboard box painted to look like a double-decker London bus.

The deputy mayor of Gijon, along with others, expressed shock and disbelief about what had happened to Connor. It was simply incomprehensible that health and social care could be so abjectly poor in a country they thought of as advanced.

You were a cute baby, matey. So blooming cute. Those cheeks. A smile to light up the neighbourhood and beyond. And that laugh...sprinklings of warm deliciousness.

Mum. Mum?

Yes?

Mum. Was I born in a bath, Mum?

Yes, you were. At home.

Mum...Mum? Did I die in a bath, Mum?

Yes.

Why, Mum?

I don't know.

CHAPTER 13

Justice for Connor Sparrowhawk and All the Young Dudes

At the heart of this story is love. A young man whose story managed to mobilise a social movement in a society in which people labelled with learning disabilities and autism are too often sidelined or ostracised. It featured a Scania truck and two red double-decker buses, a world-leading human rights team, a case discussed by the Secretary of State in the House of Commons and a campaign that was marked and celebrated by hundreds of people in the UK and beyond.

Connor wouldn't have been surprised.

He'd lift his head up from lying on his 'Connortown' mat, look up from watching YouTube at the kitchen table while basking in the sunshine, grin and repeatedly ask for details. His self-confidence was in many ways undented by the limitations imposed on him and so many others by an unfit-for-purpose system, until those last few months. Even then, I think his inner strength survived.

In a family tree drawn by a psychologist in the Unit, Connor added Dappy and Tulisa from the band N-Dubz as additional siblings and a long-lost great uncle, Lawrence. He'd started to watch *Dirty Harry* films with a couple of patients and talked about becoming a film director – his flip video camera was returned with his belongings. He'd filmed his buses, with his key nurse Winnie's voice in the background asking if he wanted to have a wash before we took him out for lunch, and a silent shot of him giving the Unit the finger. Love him.

I hope the telling of this story has also captured the inhumane battering families can be subjected to when their child, sister, brother, parent or other family member dies a preventable death in NHS or social care, and the deep inequality and inequity woven in and throughout the system. This is apparent at, for example, the level of funding legal representation but is less obvious or transparent when it comes to portraying family members or whole families as vexatious, unreasonable or worse.

We were in a privileged position in terms of our jobs, training, comfortableness with social media (for me more than Rich) and the support we were able to draw on. The writing of family life on my blog between 2011 and 2013 meant LB had an unusual personhood given the obscuring or obliteration of dehumanising processes of health and social care. At the same time this writing may have affected the treatment he received. Something that chills me to the core.

Like the still-unpublished posts I wrote in those early weeks and months after he died, some parts of what happened are too unbearable to return to. The medical records from the 107 days in the Unit, in which the only thing that came through consistently was his steadfast belief I would bring him home. I didn't.

I've not written in detail about Connor's time in the Unit for this reason. For all the made-up mother-blame shite chucked my way, I already had a lifetime supply neatly stacked up to endure.

There are other parts of our story – a settlement in a human rights case – which I've left out as being too painful, though the details are available in the public domain. We had taken him to a place that had drifted off course from what it was meant to be, sustained in its dereliction of duty by ignorance and incompetence. It might have been slightly more bearable had any of the orgnisations involved held their hands up and said sorry straight away. All failed to do this, instead going on the offensive or trying to absolve themselves of responsibility.

While it's traditional to end a book on a positive note, I have mixed feelings about the 'success' of our campaign, partly because I'm not sure we have achieved much change. We managed to generate discomfort and shine a light on things already in the public domain. Rich has said all along that we might never know what impact the death of Connor and others, as well as the campaign has had.

The 'smaller', less high-profile stuff may be deeply important but less obvious: the incorporation of Connor's and others' stories into teaching curricula, talks, presentations, book chapters and so on. We receive messages from people saying that they feel able to push for accountability for the unexpected death of their daughter, son, sister or brother because of #JusticeforLB, or from people letting us know how Connor's story has had an impact on their lives, their studies, their work.

Just one example, from a student nurse:

LB is shaping the education nurses receive. He is changing the way people work who have been nurses for years, and most important of all, LB is making the lives of other people safer and ensuring they get the care and support they need.

People still get in touch by email, Twitter or Facebook to share their experiences, and to say how sorry they are about what happened to Connor. We still hear from people who knew Connor.

This message arrived in early 2017, nearly four years after Connor's death:

Sara, you likely won't remember me – I used to work at John Watson Kids' Club (and the school too) a long time ago now (about 13–14 years ago). I came to your home and looked after your gorgeous kids a few times and loved it. :) Connor was one of my absolute favourite kids to work with and hang out with – so much personality and such a gentle, beautiful boy. I still think of him and talk about him now, he really stole a piece of my heart. I've only just discovered your blog and was devastated to read what happened to Connor. I'm so very sorry, I can't even begin to imagine how devastated you all must be. Sending you all loads of love, L. xxxx

A key theme throughout this book has been a stitching and weaving together of colour, love, brilliance and humour through unspeakable happenings – a collective creativity. We almost need to bottle this, analyse it and produce a recipe so it can be repeated by others and improved on.

The magic was, and is, that there is no recipe. There are no rules, jargon or kowtowing needed to rail against the life-beating processes and bureaucracy that shut down joy, love, sense and humanity.

In our story, we stepped up and each did what we could in myriad ways with integrity, tenacity, humour and a dose of bold. As Paul Scarrott who came on the Camino said:

'It was just really sad how Southern Health let people with learning disabilities down. I went to Connor's inquest every day because it was important. I wanted to know what was said, and I wanted them to take responsibility for what happened.'

Back in the day, me, Fran and a bunch of parents in Oxfordshire thought we were pioneering the way forward in bucking the 'misery taint' associated with learning-disabled children. We would be different. Our kids were going to lead fulfilled lives, surrounded by love, encouragement and the best we could provide. We were oblivious to the waves of parents who had come before us and who were fighting on through into their seventies and eighties, doing their very best to carve out a space for their children to lead fulfilled lives; the army of Weary Mothers and Fathers who never stop loving and battling against an inhumane system in which certain people simply do not count.

We have also, over the course of the last four years, met or been in touch with other devastated families whose learning-disabled son or daughter has died a preventable death within shite NHS and social care or, in Danny's case, Mencap provision. This is how their parents describe their children.

Richard Handley

Richard was the eldest of three children and always a much-loved member of the family. As a boy, he endeared himself to many with his engaging, friendly and mischievous personality. He was always in the thick of whatever was happening and loved to just have a go. So many happy memories of his childhood: slides, swings, climbing frame, ball games, swimming, walks, go-kart, hours carefully copying out Postman Pat stories, arranging dozens of Playmobil figures ready for action, farm visits, theme parks, favourite films and TV watching, food, hanging out with family…all spring to mind. When he was assailed by psychosis aged 18 he lost interest in many of these things but, in good times, the old Richard shone through. He could be stubborn but often for a good reason, if we could only figure out what it was. He maintained his love for family, food, his theatre group, farting, Mars bars and Coke, tickling the toes of people he liked, films, Mr Bean... He leaves a gaping hole which can never be filled.

Edward Hartley

Despite his profound learning disabilities and almost nightly seizures, Edward lived life to the fullest extent possible. He was well known for his engaging sense of fun and his big beaming smile. His was a life well lived, with the ability to always bring out the best in those he met.

Edward was a great ambassador for people with learning disabilities. Anyone meeting Edward, if only for a few minutes, would always remember him. Edward's ability to connect and communicate without saying a single word was incredible. The smile said it all. He was never judgemental; his belief in the goodness of people was a given, and this made him approachable. Not everyone has the opportunity of meeting others with a learning disability and this lack of experience often makes people nervous, but Edward would break down all the barriers by just being Edward. This was his amazing gift.

The gift of a smile is not something we think about but can be so freely given and, like Edward, it can be short lived but can have a huge impact.

Danny Tozer

Danny was a people person; he liked being part of the crowd, so pubs, clubs and cafes with a pot of tea were his favourite destinations. He loved eating out and enjoyed a varied and healthy diet, especially green veg, Marmite, peanut butter and dried fruit!

His preferred activities were physical and often outdoors, meeting sensory needs to keep moving – walking in the countryside, cycling on a trike, swimming, trampolining and horse riding. His relaxed approach on a horse led his instructor to say Danny had changed the way she taught riding. Danny also excelled at running, completing the York 10K twice in aid of International Service, winning an award for the best disabled athlete.

Music was important to Danny; in childhood listening to nursery rhymes, singing in tune with good sense of rhythm. Later, playing his piano in a percussive way peppered with a mean glissando was a great comfort.

Danny also liked travelling to new as well as familiar haunts and relished flying, cruising, trains and buses. His chosen day was a sunny seaside with fish and chips, his sister alongside.

These parents, like so many others, continue to fight for justice and accountability for the deaths of their children.

Nick Hodge, a Professor in Autism at Sheffield Hallam University, recently wrote:

> *The American political activist [Van] Jones (2016) has said that Alicia Garza in using the hashtag #blacklivesmatter changed a nation's conversation. Just as 23 years ago on 22 April 1993 the savage murder of a young man, Stephen Lawrence, did in the UK. Stephen was just waiting for a bus. Today over 1200 disabled people in the UK die needlessly each year: death by indifference (Barleon, 2013). Once again it has taken the death of a young man, Connor Sparrowhawk, or LB as he is known to many, and the heart ripped out of yet another family, to start this conversation: #disabledlivesmattertoo.*

I hope this much-needed conversation has started. We all have a responsibility to drag the UK out of a learning disability 'care' space that seems to remain aligned closer to the eugenic practices of the last century than a so-called advanced, civilised society.

We all have a right to live, love and flourish.

The Connor Manifesto

What does #JusticeforLB look like?

For LB

To achieve all of the below:

- Staff, as appropriate, to be referred to their relevant regulatory bodies.

- A corporate manslaughter prosecution brought against the Trust.

- Meaningful involvement at the inquest, and any future investigations into LB's death, so we can see the Trust and staff account for their actions in public.

For Southern Health and the local authority

- Explanation from the CCG/local authority about how they could commission such poor services.

- Reassurance about how they will ensure this cannot happen again.

- An independent investigation into the other 'natural cause' deaths in Southern Health learning disability and mental health provision over the past ten years.

For all the young dudes

- A change in the law so that every unexpected death in a 'secure' (loose definition) or locked unit automatically is investigated independently.

- Inspection/regulation: it shouldn't take catastrophic events to bring appalling professional behaviour to light. There is something about the 'hiddenness' of terrible practices that happen in full view of health and social care professionals. Both Winterbourne and STATT had external professionals in and out. LB died and a team were instantly sent in to investigate, yet nothing amiss was noticed. Improved CQC inspections could help to change this, but a critical lens is needed to examine what '(un)acceptable' practice looks like for dudes like LB.

- Prevention of the misuse/appropriation of the Mental Capacity Act as a tool to distance families and isolate young dudes.

- An effective demonstration by the NHS to make provision for learning-disabled people a complete and integral part of the health and care services provided rather than add-on, ad hoc and (easily ignored) specialist provision.

- Proper informed debate about the status of learning-disabled adults as full citizens in the UK, involving and led by learning-disabled people and their families, and what this means in terms of service provision in the widest sense and the visibility of this group as part of 'mainstream' society.

The Cast of #107daysofaction

Day	Date	Adopted by	Blog post	Action
Day 0	19/03/2014		#107days begins	
Day 1	20/03/2014		Postcards of Awesome	A collection of 107 postcards celebrating everything awesome about a person with a disability.
Day 2	21/03/2014	Sara Ryan	Happiness	A two-hour conversation discussing LB in the happy days.
Day 3	22/03/2014	A collective action of writers and editors	Letter for Connor	A letter published in *The Guardian* to coincide with the House of Lords debate on premature deaths of people with learning disabilities.
Day 4	23/03/2014		Lessons from dudes and dudettes	New blogs established to join the conversation: #JusticeforLB @WiseGrannie.
Day 5	24/03/2014	Mark Neary	Stories from an assessment and treatment unit	Mark Neary shared the awful experiences his son Steven experienced titled '107 stories from Steven's time in an assessment and treatment unit'.
Day 6	25/03/2014	Katie Peacock	Two communities respond	Katie Peacock shared her thoughts on why she adopted a day from #107days. Day 6 saw the coming together of two small Yorkshire villages to connect people and raise awareness for the campaign.
Day 7	26/03/2014	Sukey Carder	Hair raising support	Sukey Carder of Sukey's Hair Lounge used one of LB's postcards to inspire one of her models competing in a charity hair show. The money raised from the event was for an epilepsy charity.

Day 8	27/03/2014	Zinnia and Kay	Growing awareness	Zinnia is a horticultural social enterprise that held a day where volunteers plant stock and the money raised was donated to LB's fighting fund, established to cover legal costs.
				Kay attended the Lincolnshire Autistic Society annual conference where she took some of LB's postcards to raise awareness.
Day 9	28/03/2014	Fiona Fisher	Beach art	A creative portrait of a big bus was drawn on the sands of a beach in Fife.
Day 10	29/03/2014	Michelle Dudderidge	Hands in Hands with AL	Michelle shared the story of AL and his journey from being an unkempt, lost and scared man in an assessment and treatment unit to being a happy young dude receiving the right support.
Day 11	30/03/2014	Shelley Mason	A mother's thoughts	Shelley posted why, as a mother and a human being, she felt Justice for LB was important.
Day 12	31/03/2014	Beth Gregson	Spreading the word to Healthwatch	Beth brought Justice for LB to the attention of Healthwatch in the hope of raising the profile for what is happening in terms of support for people with learning disabilities.
Day 13	01/04/2014	Bringing Us Together	Bringing Us Together chat	Bringing Us Together is a parent-driven company that aims to bring parents, young people, family and practitioners together to share learning and resources. It showed its support by giving Sara a chance to chat about the campaign via its site.
Day 14	02/04/2014	Damian Milton	Moments in time	Day 14 falls on World Autism Day. Damian used the day by raising awareness for the campaign, making a request for others to join him in supporting Justice for LB and in accepting all autistic people.

Day	Date	Adopted by	Blog post	Action
Day 15	03/04/2014	Foundation for People with Learning Difficulties and WeLDNurses	Focusing on the person	A joint Twitter chat between these two organisations, which provided service users, parents, carers and learning disability nurses with an opportunity to chat together.
Day 16	04/04/2014	Two sisters, Theresa and Ruth (not their real names)	Ruth's story	Theresa and Ruth were touched by LB's story and wanted to share a positive experience of an assessment unit.
Day 17	05/04/2014	Adam and Meraud	A dude named Adam	Adam and Meraud wanted to support Justice for LB by sharing LB's enthusiasm for buses in taking a mammoth tour of Brighton on a bendy bus. They also travelled to London (also loved by LB) with a local youth group. Meraud and Adam share their story of hope and possibility.
Day 18	06/04/2014	Ruth Whiteside	A marathon for Connor and Hope	Ruth ran 26.2 miles in the Hardmoors Wainstones Trail marathon, with Connor and her daughter Hope, another awesome dudette, as her inspiration.
Day 19	07/04/2014	Sam Sly	Assessment and treatment units (ATUs) – a tweet a day	Sam shared her passion for those with learning disabilities and mental health issues by tweeting every day for 107 days.
Day 20	08/04/2014	Amanda Reynolds	What's a board to do?	Amanda offered her support to Justice for LB by giving us an insight into her experience working on the NHS boards and she shared a post on what an NHS board member is there to do.

Day	Date	Name	Title	Description
Day 21	09/04/2014	Deborah Faulkner	Looking forward to the weekend	Deborah ran the London Marathon and decided to dedicate her run to the Justice for LB campaign after discovering it on Facebook.
Day 22	10/04/2014	Rebecca	Coastal horizons	Rebecca shares a little reflection of Connor's life in a blog post.
Day 23	11/04/2014	The Tizard Centre	Jim Mansell Memorial Lecture	Tizard is an academic group at the University of Kent whose work is centred on learning disability and community care. Patricia Howlin, Professor of Clinical Psychology, delivered the Jim Mansell Memorial Lecture, named after the founder of the Tizard Centre. The lecture began with a video that celebrated the life of LB.
Day 24	12/04/2014	Lucy Skye	An Exmoor marathon	Lucy ran the Exmoor marathon to raise awareness of LB and the treatment of many like him.
Day 25	13/04/2014		Taking stock	Day 25 celebrated all the amazing activities that have taken place during 107 days of action.
Day 26	14/04/2014	First Note	First notes of empowerment	First Note is an all-ability music group based in London, which stands for all people with varying abilities and disabilities having a voice. First Note wrote, sang and recorded a song in support of Justice for LB.
Day 27	15/04/2014	Anne-Marie Boylan and Louise Locock	Lamentations for LB	Anne-Marie and Louise sang in the mediavel chapel of Bartlemas in Oxford where they sang a collection of poetic laments that seemed all too appropriate for Justice for LB.
Day 28	16/04/2014	Kara	Drops of brilliance	Kara is mother to Grenouille, who has a rare genetic rearrangement. Kara adopted this day by sharing her motivation to get involved with Justice for LB.

Day	Date	Adopted by	Blog post	Action
Day 29	17/04/2014	Charlotte	Spreading joy	Charlotte is passionate about improving the services for people with learning disabilities and decided to adopt this day and share a blog post portraying her exploits.
Day 30	18/04/2014	Andreas Dimopolous	What would you do?	Andreas is a researcher who is passionate about disability rights and wanted to share his thoughts on the death of LB.
Day 31	19/04/2014	Madi Barnicoat	Paddling for Justice for LB	Madi participated in the Canoeist's Everest boat race, paddling 125 miles in just over four days to raise money for the LB fighting fund.
Day 32	20/04/2014	Lucy Series	Recognising support	Lucy offered to adopt this day and blog for #107daysofaction. The post provides context and information about the Mental Capacity Act and the role that families can play. The post also advises family members on what they can do if they feel shut out.
Day 33	21/04/2014	Sara Ryan	Fulfilling ambitions	Sara wrote a post reflecting on LB's future as this day celebrated the fact that a number of LB's ambitions have been met.
Day 34	22/04/2014	Sara Ryan	What sociological imagination?	LB's mum presented at the postgraduate pre-event for #BritSoc14 in Leeds, which she dedicated to LB. Sara chatted with postgraduate students asking them why they think learning-disabled people are ignored and marginalised in sociological research.
Day 35	23/04/2014	Louise	ATUs, autism and anxiety	Louise adopted this day to share some of her thoughts on assessment and treatment units and their suitability (or not) for people with autism.

Day 36	24/04/2014	Sarah	Cry me a river Katrina Percy	Sarah is a Canadian blogger, freelance writer and disability advocate who adopted this day to share LB's story and raise awareness of the campaign in Canada and in the USA.
Day 37	25/04/2014	Sally Donovan	When care goes missing	Sally adopted this day to share a blog post on absent care and compassion.
Day 38	26/04/2014	Big Man's Mum	Happy Birthday, Big Man	Big Man's mum used this day to share a post celebrating some positives.
Day 39	27/04/2014		Still time to get involved	This post encouraged people to get involved and support #107days, and suggested how people could participate, for example by sharing events and activities.
Day 40	28/04/2014	Ermintrude	Musings from the Magic Roundabout	Ermintrude shares her thoughts and musings on day 40 in support of Justice for LB.
Day 41	29/04/2014	Fiona	A question of trust	Fiona adopted this day by raising her concerns for the future, questioning how we can trust the NHS.
Day 42	30/04/2014	Phil Brayshaw	A day in the life of...	Phil is a registered nurse for people with learning disabilities. He shared a post he wrote in memory of LB, in the hope that it encourages at least one person to do one thing differently.
Day 43	01/05/2014	WeLDNurses	Death by indifference	As part of #107days, WeLDNurses adopted this day for the second of three web chats where the discussion was centred on the topic 'Death by indifference'.

Day	Date	Adopted by	Blog post	Action
Day 44	02/05/2014	Lauren	Healthy one-page profiles	Lauren adopted this day by sharing a post building on the discussion from days 42 and 43.
Day 45	03/05/2014	Rodgers Coaches and Earthline LTD	The fleet keeps growing	This day celebrated LB's passion for transport and his long-standing dream to have a company called ConnorCo. Rodgers Coaches made Connor's dream a reality by dedicating three red double-decker school buses to him. LB's auntie Sam contacted a local transport company, Earthline, to name a lorry after him, which it did! Another dream comes true!
Day 46	04/05/2014	Katherine Runswick-Cole and Dan Goodley	The violence of disablism	Katherine and Dan wrote a post together on the Violence of Disablism based on their published academic paper on the topic. Katherine shared this paper in Norway.
Day 47	05/05/2014	Saba Salman	Indignation and initiative vs 'institutional inertia'	Saba wrote the initial piece on LB's death and #JusticeforLB, published in *The Guardian* on Day 0. She adopted today by writing a post for 107 Days of Action.
Day 48	06/05/2014	Angela Broadbridge	Speaking up and speaking out	Angela shared her thoughts on why she got involved and supported 107 days, and she also wrote a blog post reflecting on her work around advocacy, referencing Sara's attempts to advocate for LB.
Day 49	07/05/2014	Hannah Morgan and Chris Hatton from the Centre for Disability Research, Lancaster University	An academic point?	Hannah and Chris organised, presented and live-tweeted two events. The first event was a lecture on institutional abuse and the second was a seminar entitled 'Laughing Boy versus the Zombie Institution: Closing the New Institutions for People with Learning Disabilities'.

Day 50	08/05/2014	Jill Smith	Care essentials?	Jill adopted the day by building on the academic efforts from day 49.
Day 51	09/05/2014	Jane Youell	107k for #107days	Jane shared her support for LB by running 107k through 11 consecutive days.
Day 52	10/05/2014	Pippa Murray	Afternoon tea	Pippa from ibk initiatives adopted the day by hosting an afternoon tea for disabled children, young people, family, friends and personal assistants. The special occasion raised awareness about Justice for LB. A mosaic artist was invited to put together an art piece where everyone could take part; the letters 'LB' were included in honour of Connor.
Day 53	11/05/2014	Sara Ryan	The golden M(iddle)	A positive reflection of the 107 days of action so far.
Day 54	12/05/2014	N/A	N/A	Rest day
Day 55	13/05/2014	Paradigm and friends Sally Warren, Jayne Knight and Nan Carle	Connecting voices	The day was spent in a community workshop, facilitated by Paradigm and was focused on connecting the voices of people from around the country to highlight injustice. LB was with the group throughout the day, with a symbolic empty chair.
Day 56	14/05/2014	Inclusion North	Citizen power	Inclusion North's Board of Directors and Advisory Council talked about what happened to LB and what has happened since he died. Inclusion North wanted to do something that helped other people have their say and get involved.
Day 57	15/05/2014	John Williams	My son's not Rainman	John is a comedian and single dad whose son is autistic. John showed his support to the #107days campaign by sharing his thoughts on his blog.

Day	Date	Adopted by	Blog post	Action
Day 58	16/05/2014	Kabie, Pam and Geraldine	Different, not less	Kabie, Pam and Geraldine, and autism rights group Highland, adopted today by using it to raise awareness about Connor and #JusticeforLB at their Autism and Ethics conference.
Day 59	17/05/2014	Janis Firminger, Margaret Taylor and Janet Read	Time and place	Janis, Margaret and Janet exhibited their art work at their Time and Place textile exhibition. One of the pieces in the exhibition was made in memory of Connor. The three also celebrated LB's life, raising awareness for the campaign by making LB's justice quilt.
Day 60	18/05/2014	Beck	107 red balloons	Beck from Frog Orange welcomed people to Shotover where 107 red balloons were released in memory of LB.
Day 61	19/05/2014	Lucy Series, Cardiff Law School	Justice – one stitch at a time	At Cardiff Law School, a creative seminar was held as part of 107 Days of Action. The seminar explained what had happened to Connor, describing some of the wider justice issues affecting people with learning disabilities. Around 30 students and staff in Cardiff spent a few hours stitching, gluing, knitting and drawing on patches for the justice quilt in honour of LB.
Day 62	20/05/2014	Nikki, John and Andre	Learning Disabilities Elves get to work	Nikki, John and Andre are behind the Learning Disabilities Elf blog, which contains videos, databases, journals and so on to identify what is important to professionals working with people with learning disabilities in health or social care. They released a post in support of Justice for LB.
Day 63	21/05/2014	Adam	An EP for LB	Adam got together with his friend Marc to recreate some of Connor's favourite songs to raise money and awareness for the campaign. The duo recorded a covers EP featuring four of LB's top songs.

Day	Date	Name	Title	Description
Day 64	22/05/2014	Zoe	A jewel of a future	Zoe joined the Justice for LB and 107 days campaign after being awakened to the horrors of ATUs. To raise money towards the costs of legal representation at Connor's inquest, Zoe participated in running a jewellery party to raise funds.
Day 65	23/05/2014	Mark Sherry	Solidarity sent from Toledo	Mark, his students, their family, friends and community members in Ohio shared their solidarity with Justice for LB by creating a video to share LB's story and raise awareness.
Day 66	24/05/2014	Sharon, Heather and the Oxford Woodcraft Folk	Woodcrafting buses	Woodcraft Folk is the co-operative children and young people's movement committed to promoting inclusion, respect and social justice. The young people were moved by the #JusticeforLB campaign and shared their compassion and support through drawings.
Day 67	25/05/2014	Amanda Boorman	The clients are revolting	Amanda, founder of The Open Nest, shared her thoughts, feelings and experiences as a professional, a mother and a supporter of #JusticeforLB.
Day 68	26/05/2014	Beckie Whelton	Get a move on	Beckie adopted a day to use at her local messy church service where the children in the service spent time making quilt patches for Connor. In the service that followed, awareness was raised about what happened to Connor and everyone left with a flyer and the knowledge of how to donate to the fighting fund.
Day 69	27/05/2014	Lois	The importance of listening	Lois adopted day 69 because she felt her experience in communication was relevant to #JusticeforLB and the way that people with learning disabilities experience the health service. Lois has worked alongside a diverse group of people with a range of communication support needs where, together, they developed an interactive workbook for NHS Education Scotland.

Day	Date	Adopted by	Blog post	Action
Day 70	28/05/2014	Yvonne Newbold	Shadows of action	Yvonne adopted this day by writing a blog post sharing her personal reflections on LB and Sara's experience, and the similarities to those of her and her son Toby. Yvonne shared pictures of the LB fighting fund's party tickets.
Day 71	29/05/2014	WeLDNurses	WeLDNurses finale	Today was the third and final Twitter chat in conjunction with WeLDNurses.
Day 72	30/05/2014	Tom Shakespeare	Enabling equality	Tom gave the BSA/British Library annual Equality lecture and used the opportunity to dedicate the lecture to LB.
Day 73	31/05/2014	Caroline Jordan and Carrie Morgan	His life honoured	Day 73 was the party night where there was a choice between an English country dance or the LB Fighting Fund Party. Caroline Jordan organised the country dance with a few others in honour of LB to raise awareness in solidarity of the campaign. Carrie Morgan adopted the day on her birthday, and she shared a short poem.
Day 74	01/06/2014	Fiona Quigley	Letting the light in	Fiona, an eLearning designer and video producer from Northern Ireland, showed solidarity with this movement by creating a short documentary on supporting people with learning disabilities.
Day 75	02/06/2014	Louise	Pockets of peace	Louise adopted this day by taking Sara out to do something nice and enjoy a well-deserved treat.

Day	Date	Name	Title	Description
Day 76	03/06/2014	Aisling Duffy and the team at Certitude	Airing views	Certitude provides personalised support for people with learning disabilities, autism and mental health needs. It held an internal round-table session to reflect on what lessons could be learned from Connor's death and to address how we best support people with epilepsy, balancing both safety and independence. It also discussed how to ensure that families are central to the support provided for their relative.
Day 77	04/06/2014	Liz Thackray	Six degrees of separation	Liz offered her thoughts on how six degrees of separation can be used to support #107days and #JusticeforLB by challenging people to share LB's story with anyone they can think of in a demand for more caring and responsible support systems.
Day 78	05/06/2014	Rachel Batchelor	Pass it on	Rachel Batchelor offered to raise awareness by discussing LB's case with 107 people, asking them to discuss it with at least one other person.
Day 79	06/06/2014	Ulla	Buses, cake and prosecco	Ulla adopted this day to help more people hear Connor's story by hosting a 'Buses, Cake and Prosecco' event at The Nuffield Department of Primary Care Health Sciences, Oxford.
Day 80	07/06/2014	John	Busking for justice	Adopted by John, who knew Connor very well. In honour of LB, John played some songs in remembrance of him.
Day 81	08/06/2014	Izzi Crowther	We won't ever stop the bus	Izzi built on John's post from day 80 and shared a personal perspective of Connor's story in support of the campaign. She also shared a few links to performances worth checking out.

Day	Date	Adopted by	Blog post	Action
Day 82	09/06/2014	The partnership steering group (PSG) of the Learning Disabilities Studies Course at Manchester	Challenging attitudes, changing lives	The PSG adopted this day for its conference, 'Learning Disability Studies in Academia: Challenging Attitudes, Changing Lives'. The conference explored how learning disability studies can make a real difference to the lives of learning-disabled people.
Day 83	10/06/2014	The Housing and Support Alliance (H&SA) / British Institute of Learning Disability (BILD)	H&SA and BILD respond	Alicia from H&SA and Ann from BILD shared their reasons for choosing to get involved with supporting #107days and #JusticeforLB.
Day 84	11/06/2014	Chrissie Rogers	Mothering in the extreme	Chrissie gave a seminar for staff and students at Aston University in support of the #107days campaign. The seminar was entitled 'Mothering in the Extreme: Death, Disability and Dehumanisation'.
Day 85	12/06/2014	Martin Coyle of True Voice and Teresa of SWAN Advocacy	Advocacy actions	Both SWAN and True Voice held events, each seeking to show the important role of advocacy in keeping people at the heart of decision making and support.
Day 86	13/06/2014	Jenny Morris	Communication and being human	Jenny adopted this day to share a blog post with her thoughts and knowledge on communication. She has blogged early on in the campaign and has been interviewed by journalists to discuss a number of her pieces relating to LB.

	Date	Name	Theme	Description
Day 87	14/06/2014	Educational Rights Alliance (ERA) and Carol Stott	Letters and buses	ERA drafted a letter that people could use to send to their MP, informing them of the concerns around the use of assessment and treatment units. Carol travelled around London on as many London buses as possible to take 107 photos for a bus collage. She did this to raise awareness and funds for Justice for LB.
Day 88	15/06/2014	Marianne SB and her three children, Jacob, Izzi and Alex	A sibling manifesto	Marianne adopted the day by spending time with her children Jacob and Izzie, discussing Alex's future. Marianne showed her support for all the awesome dudes and dudettes and their siblings too.
Day 89	16/06/2014	Lisa Hinton	Calling for candour	Lisa wanted to raise awareness of what happened to Connor and the failings of the health and social care system in responding to his death. She did this by contacting an expert in patient safety, who has been explicit in the need for candour in cases such as LB's.
Day 90	17/06/2014	Eilionoir Flynn and colleagues at the Centre for Disability Law & Policy at the National University of Ireland, Galway	Voice and choice	This day was adopted as part of the centre's sixth international Disability Law Summer School. A day of the summer school was dedicated to LB as the school's focus was on access to justice and political participation for people with disabilities.
Day 91	18/06/2014	Lisa Trigg, Jo Moriarty and the Care Quality Commission (CQC)	Lunching for LB and Three Lives	Lisa and Jo met at a social care curry event and organised a gathering of people from their London School of Economics and King's College research unit. The gathering included lunch and an informal discussion in support of Justice for LB and 107 days. The CQC adopted this day as it coincided with the launch of its Three Lives report. The report featured LB's story, and the stories of Kayleigh and Lisa, two dudettes who spent time in an ATU.

Day	Date	Adopted by	Blog post	Action
Day 92	19/06/2014	Inclusion East	Inclusion East	Inclusion East is a small, committed bunch of people with complex needs, and their families and good friends. Inclusion East dedicated its monthly directors' meeting in June to discussing Justice for LB.
Day 93	20/06/2014	Steve Hardy	London buses	Steve, a consultant nurse, used his adopted day to do a very special challenge for #JusticeforLB. Steve explored Connor's love for buses by completing 107 bus journeys in one day across London.
Day 94	21/06/2014	Barbara Perry and Gail Hanrahan	Citizen Advocacy and Education Fest	The day was shared by Barbara and Gail, who wrote blog posts in support of 107 days and Justice for LB. Barbara used her blog space to promote citizen advocacy and discuss abuse. Gail's post discussed person-centred approaches and their role in ensuring good support for all dudes.
Day 95	22/06/2014	Lesley, Glynis and Emma, and Debs	Team Triathlon and Walking the Talk	Lesley, Glynis and Emma took part in the Henley Team Triathlon, where they dedicated the day to Connor. Debs supported the campaign by writing a blog post and creating a short film to campaign for a difference.
Day 96	23/06/2014	Brigid Greaney and Kathy Liddell	Oxford Bus Museum	In honour of Connor, Brigid and Kathy gathered together dudes and dudettes at one of LB's favourite places.
Day 97	24/06/2014	Gina Aylward and her son Jack	Jack's cats for justice	Gina and Jack decided that they wanted to support #JusticeforLB, so Jack made figures of small cats out of recycled materials to sell. The money raised was used for the campaign.

	Date	Names	Title	Description
Day 98	25/06/2014	Deborah Coles, Selen Cavcav and colleagues at INQUEST	An INQUEST intervention	INQUEST co-ordinated a meeting with Andrew Smith, Deborah Coles, Selen Cavcav and Sara Ryan as part of the 107 days campaign. The meeting discussed a number of urgent issues arising from Connor's death.
Day 99	26/06/2014	CHANGE and Oxfordshire Family Support Network (OxFSN)	Local experiences, national concerns	CHANGE and OxFSN are two organisations that seek to improve the provision for people with learning disabilities. CHANGE held its national event on this day, together with Lumos, for people with learning disabilities. The event aims at freeing adults, young people and children from institutions in the UK and across Europe. OxFSN, together with Healthwatch Oxfordshire, launched its new report, *A local experience of national concern*, which they dedicated to LB's memory.
Day 100	27/06/2014	Dan Goodley, Rebecca Lawthom, Ruby Goodley and Rosa Goodley	JusticeforLB hits Glastonbury	The Goodley family adopted this day by sharing their support of the campaign at the Glastonbury music festival. They publicised #JusticeforLB at the festival with a big flag and flyers.
Day 101	28/06/2014	Trish Burns and David Harling	An animated, poetic call to act	Trish supported the campaign by creating a poem in memory of LB – a creative prompt for us to act. David crafted a very personal interpretation of what happened to LB, which can be found on YouTube. The video is his personal interpretation of Connor's journey through the ATU, prompting us to act and respond!
Day 102	29/06/2014	Jemma, Simon and Eseld / Martin, Chris and John	Three cyclists and a christening	As Jemma and Simon christened their daughter Eseld, they decided to use this day in honour of LB too by making all of their friends and family aware of the campaign while raising funds also. Martin, Chris and John decided to cycle 107 miles for 107 days. The trio raised awareness and funds for the campaign.

Day	Date	Adopted by	Blog post	Action
Day 103	30/06/2014	Max Neill from the UK Learning Community for Person-Centred Practices	Person-centred practice, nursing students and a legal webchat	At the national gathering of the UK Learning Community for Person-Centred Practices, Connor's story was made known to everyone present. They shared a #JusticeforLB postcard and invited the participants to pledge in sharing how they would use their postcard, and how they would ensure that people and their families were listened to.
		Bridget Penhale and Sarah Richardson from the School of Nursing Sciences at the University of East Anglia		Bridget and Sarah ensured that a large number of staff and students at their university heard LB's story. They dedicated an undergraduate module and The Enquiry Based Learning Package to Connor.
		Steve Broach from Doughty Street Chambers		Steve is a barrister who held a free web Q&A session on the law in relation to education, health and care services for disabled young people in England.
Day 104	01/07/2014	Sunnyside Rural Trust	Voices to be heard	Sunnyside Rural Trust adopted the day by sharing a report of the celebration and launch of a special memorial garden in which 18 dudes and dudettes worked.
		Bringing Us Together		Bringing Us Together collaborated with The Cameron Trust and the Centre for Welfare Reform to give families an opportunity to come together and share their stories.
		In Control		In Control started its day with a presentation by two parents who shared their stories of the challenges of the system and the resilience needed to keep going.

Day 105	02/07/2014	Briony	In support of #107days and the Justice for LB campaign, Briony made a beautiful wall hanging centred around Connor's favourite songs.
		Mark and Sara	Mark, the Chief Executive of the National Autistic Society, adopted day 105 to write a challenging letter to himself and other social care providers.
		George Julian	George shaved her head to raise awareness and funds for her local hospice, Rowcroft, that supported her family, and for #JusticeforLB.
Day 106	03/07/2014	Laurie and Sara's colleagues, Jo, Adam and Luis	Laurie, a 53-year-old person with Asperger syndrome who has children on the autism spectrum, adopted day 106 by writing a blogpost and asking for donations for LB's fighting fund.
			Laurie was interviewed by Sara for Healthtalkonline where a team from Healthtalkonline adopted this day as a charity by sharing an interview done the day before Connor's death. The interview showed Sara talking about Connor and what an awesome dude he was.
Day 107	04/07/2014		This day marked the end of 107 Days of Action and it was exactly one year from this point that Connor died an entirely preventable death in the care of Southern Health.
			People were invited to leave a comment on the blog post to share what they took away from #107days. They were also invited to change their social media profile pictures to LB for the day in memory of him and to raise awareness of LB's campaign.

Textile art, provider challenge and a headshave

Talking and remembering

Honouring LB

Acknowledgements

Gawd. Where to start here. There is literally a cast of hundreds, many of whom have already been mentioned. I'll divvy up those who have fallen outside of a mention in the main text to acknowledge here.

Behind the scenes fairies: My younger sister, Sam, who did her best to get Eddie Stobart to name a lorry after Connor and persuaded Earthline to do so. She also travelled over weekly in the months after Connor's death to simply be there and do a cracking number on sorting out our garden.

My mate Ulla, who must have spent weeks engaging with desperate late-night emails and messages long before and after Connor's death, always responding, listening and loving. Her daughters, my goddaughter, Kerttu, and older sister, Ilona, somehow manage to fill a love space with effortless deliciousness.

Beth Hill, Jane Iliffe, Nicola Anderton and others from Oxford Brookes who packaged us off to Devon for a weekend away that first year, and Abbey Halcli who was a fab inquest ally and more.

Funmi Akinola for doing such a thorough job producing the #107daysofaction table.

The Davis family for consistently anticipating gaps with home-cooked food and daily dog walking in those early months and our other friends and neighbours who just get it and act.

Matt Wellstead who produced the #JusticeforLB flyer and everyone who contributed to the crowdsourced legal fees for Connor's inquest. It's outrageous that families are not entitled to legal representation in this situation, but people stepped up in their hundreds, and I'm sorry we've not been able to write to or thank you individually.

Social media fairies: There are an army of you lot who are too numerous to mention. I just wanted to say that each and every blog comment, tweet, retweet, expression of rage and love and more has been appreciated and stoked the 'we can do this' power. The specialist knowledge we've been able to tap into has been invaluable and I love the enthusiastic nerdiness and generosity of so many people from so many different backgrounds.

Book writing fairies: Jenny Hislop, a friend and colleague, who encouraged and coaxed me to write and criticised an early version resoundingly. 'No one wants to read angry' was one memorable comment over a glass of vino or two. She also drew on various publishing contacts to provide further advice. Other early book tasters with sense and forthright comments included Liz Ellis, Helen Salisbury and Kirsty Keywood.

The Jessica Kingsley Publishers team, particularly Stephen Jones and Emma Holak, who were beyond patient with my holding this baby close and not wanting to let go of it.

Work: The unexpected and preventable death of a family member is an unspeakable experience. To have a work environment in which this is not only recognised but also generates a seamless and stress-free withdrawal from work commitments has been priceless. To the department, I stand in admiration that you never once even hinted that I should tone down the language or content of my social media activity. To colleagues who picked up my work without hesitation or murmur, I thank you.

And finally, a couple of cheeky re-mentions.

George Julian, I take my hat off to your remarkable campaigning skills, tenacity and commitment to social justice, which involved countless hours of unpaid work, given cheerfully and with a lot of laughs. You were the, too often unseen, brains behind the operation.

Rich, Rosie, Will, Owen and Tom: I just bloody love you so much. This love and the pride that comes with it is probably the glue that holds together the pieces of my heart. Thank you.